39 NEW SAINTS YOU SHOULD KNOW

39
new
SAINTS
you
should
know

Brian O'Neel

FOREWORD BY JOSEPH PEARCE

SERVANT
BOOKS

PUBLISHED BY ST. ANTHONY MESSENGER PRESS
CINCINNATI, OHIO

Cover and book design by Mark Sullivan
Cover image copyright ©Shutterstock/Fenton

LIBRARY OF CONGRESS CATALOGING-IN-PUBLICATION DATA
O'Neel, Brian.
39 new saints you should know / Brian O'Neel.
p. cm.
Includes bibliographical references and index.
ISBN 978-0-86716-928-7 (pbk. : alk. paper) 1. Christian saints—Biography. I. Title. II. Title: Thirty nine new saints you should know.
BX4655.3.O54 2010
282.092′2—dc22
[B]
2010008923

ISBN 978-0-86716-928-7

Published by Servant Books, an imprint of St. Anthony Messenger Press.
28 W. Liberty St.
Cincinnati, OH 45202
www.AmericanCatholic.org
www.ServantBooks.org

Printed in the United States of America.

Printed on acid-free paper.

10 11 12 13 14 5 4 3 2 1

To my wife, Karyn, and our children—
Michael, John Patrick, Kaitlin, Aidan, Eilis, Liam,
and any who follow—to whom I owe an immeasurable debt.

Acknowledgments

To Mike Aquilina, who has been so kind and who introduced me to my editor, Cindy Cavnar, which led to this book. To Cindy herself, whose firm hand made this a better book. To Joseph Pearce for his thoughtful foreword. To Denise Kramer, Rebecca Long, Karen McClelland, Mary de la Cruz, Lisa Pruitt McCoy, Virginia "Ginny" Hodal, Rose Schumer, and Joe Pursch for looking over the manuscript and offering excellent suggestions. To Bob Yerkes: Thank you for opening my eyes.

To the postulators and vice postulators of causes who responded to my voluminous questions. To our recent popes, especially John Paul II, for bringing the Church so many blesseds and saints. Most especially to our Lord Jesus Christ for the gift of salvation, to his Blessed Mother for her prayers and maternal guidance, and to St. Joseph for his loving patronage.

Foreword

On May 16, 2004, I had the honor and privilege to be at St. Peter's in Rome, along with my wife, Susannah, our two-year-old son, Leo, and our unborn daughter, Gianna, for the canonization of St. Gianna Beretta Molla and five others by John Paul II. What a joy to be present at such a glorious event! I felt that if our own Gianna had been big enough (she was only a few weeks old at the time), she would have emulated St. John the Baptist by leaping for joy in her mother's womb at the sheer wonder of being in the presence of Christ on such a holy occasion. Her parents expressed her joy vicariously as we witnessed the mystical birth of a saint who is an icon of modern motherhood and the culture of life.

St. Gianna Beretta Molla is but one of a heavenly host of recently canonized or beatified holy men and women who are brought together in this volume by Brian O'Neel. This is a book filled to the brim, filled to bursting, with sanctity and with shining examples of the nobility of virtue. In an age that shuns nobility and vilifies virtue, the men and women who emerge from these pages are countercultural heroes and heroines, showing us the way through the darkness of the culture of death in the presence of the Source of all life.

As a means of introducing some of the holy men and women who bless these pages, I'm going to indulge myself (and beg the reader's indulgence) with a personal selection of some of my own favorites among them. In doing so I must begin by confessing the sins of omission that accompany such self-indulgence and invite the reader to discover the other saints and blesseds within this volume for themselves.

Apart from obvious favorites, such as Mother Teresa and Padre Pio (to give them their less grandiose, noncanonized names), I have a particular devotion to Pope (now Blessed) Pius IX. What a defiant opponent of regressive "progress," and what an indefatigably courageous defender of the Church against the rise of secular fundamentalism! Along with St. Pius X and Popes Pius XI and XII, Bl. Pius IX is one of the four "pious" pillars upon which (under grace) the Church's resistance to communism, modernism, Nazism, and liberal eugenics rests securely.

I'm delighted that the Emperor Karl I has been beatified. His example of true Christian kingship—that is, kingship as service, kingship that subjects itself in humility to the needs of its subjects—is an image of the kingship of Christ and renders Karl worthy, therefore, of his place among the blessed at Christ's right hand.

It is also gratifying to see the beatification of those martyred at the hands of communism and other anti-Catholic regimes. Bl. Vicente Vilar David, one of thousands of Christians killed by communist and anarchist Republicans in the Spanish Civil War, kept the most difficult of our Lord's commandments, loving his enemies even as they were about to shoot him in cold blood. "I forgive you" were his immortal last words. Bl. Miguel Pro's last words, uttered with his arms stretched out like Christ on the cross as he faced his executioners, were *"Viva Cristo Rey!"*—"Long live Christ the King!" These were also the last words fourteen-year-old José Luis Sánchez del Río exclaimed as he was being repeatedly stabbed by Mexican soldiers.

Another martyr, though of a somewhat different sort, is Bl. Laura Vicuña, described by Brian O'Neel as "the other Maria Goretti." Laura suffered sexual and physical abuse, eventually dying of her injuries. And last but not least, how can we fail to mention Louis and Zélie Martin, the now beatified parents of St. Thérèse of Lisieux, who have rightly become icons of marital love and the self-sacrificial Christian parenthood that puts Planned Parenthood to shame?

This is but a sprinkling of the sparkling firmament of holiness that Brian O'Neel presents to us. In turning the pages that follow, you will be entering into an adventure that offers many new heroes and heroines. You will have your imagination baptized by their blood, your faith fortified by their courage, your hope heartened by their deeds, and your love enflamed by their passion. And most importantly, as confirmed by their beatification or canonization by the Church, you will know that they are able to intercede for you at God's right hand.

Deo gratias! Viva Cristo Rey!

Joseph Pearce

Introduction

Bl. Pope John XXIII once told a story from his days as a young seminarian in Rome. He and his friends had hired a cab to take them to St. Peter's Square so they could stand vigil with the other faithful while Pope Leo XIII lay dying.

"The coachman was still the pulse of public opinion at that time," the pope related. "Without much encouragement, the cabbie expressed his opinion freely: 'I think Leo XIII is the greatest pope of all time. When he dies, he will, of course, be replaced, but I will be very surprised if the new one attracts as many pilgrims to Rome. No other pope will ever give us coachmen so much work and so much bread as Leo XIII.'"

After relaying this story, John is said to have smiled and concluded, "And therein lies the greatness of Leo XIII."[1]

If this is true of Leo, what would our cabbie have said about John Paul II or Benedict XVI? John Paul II's general audiences and Angelus addresses drew millions over the course of his twenty-four-year pontificate. In 2003 my wife and I made our first trip to Rome precisely to see him. Later his funeral attracted an estimated five to seven million pilgrims. Benedict is attracting such large crowds that he is on pace to outdraw John Paul II. Indeed, more people came to see him in the first year of his pontificate than came to Rome during the 2000 Jubilee Year.

But it is the making of saints that arguably drew the most people to the Eternal City. John Paul II canonized 482 saints and beatified 1,338 individuals. Most of these ceremonies were held in Rome in St. Peter's Square, bringing sometimes hundreds of thousands of men and women from around the world to the heart of Christendom.

With such daunting numbers of recently canonized and beatified figures, you can be excused for not knowing many of them. Oh, sure, there are the famous ones, such as Opus Dei founder St. Josemaría Escrivá, the Divine Mercy visionary St. Faustina, Bl. Mother Teresa of Calcutta, and St. Padre Pio. By and large, however, the saints and blesseds of recent years are wholly unfamiliar.

And this is a shame, because some of these men and women have simply amazing stories. Furthermore, these stories show us something. They show us the way to holiness, but more importantly, they show that sanctity is the only thing worth having, the only thing that gives our life any real meaning. They also show us that sainthood is for everyone and not just the boring pursuit of a halo and a harp to strum on in the clouds for eternity. Rather, holiness is thrilling, because it is the pursuit of God, who is more exciting than anything this world can ever offer. Pursuit of a life in him is the true extreme sport.

That is not to say that each one of these men and women was faster than a speeding bullet or leapt tall buildings in a single bound. Many who knew them during their lifetimes might be surprised that we are still thinking about them. But whether they were fearless martyrs, amazing priests, dedicated religious, humble servants of the poor, innovative catechists, or everyday working men and women, they were all incredible and truly exemplary people. Each of us would be proud to say we know such people.

Speaking of martyrs, in Western countries the right to worship as we wish is ingrained in our collective DNA. We can be excused, therefore, for thinking that martyrdom for the faith happened only back in Roman times. "Apostatize or die" is not a demand we can imagine these days, is it? Yet the fact is that more Christians lost their lives for their faith in the twentieth century than in all the previous nineteen centuries combined. And in places such as North Korea, China, and Iraq, martyrdoms still occur.

The Church has raised to the altar many who were slain for their faith in the last century. They stand as witnesses of the courage we need to stand firm in the face of secularism, the culture of death, and other evil forces.

A note to keep in mind as you read this book: Mother Angelica has often said that there is a warm place in purgatory for hagiographers who write glorified saint stories. You know the ones: They have made this or that saint seem impossibly holy. I have relatives who don't read saints' stories because they *all* seem like that. Of St. Aloysius Gonzaga, for instance, some say that he never looked at his mother, as if that somehow made him holy. Other hagiographers write that St. Bernard of Clairvaux didn't know what the ceiling of his monastery's chapel looked liked because his eyes were always fixed on the floor in prayer.

Now, who can identify with someone like that? More to the point, who is inspired by someone like that?

The Servant of God Fulton Sheen told a much more interesting story about St. Bernard. He was going down a road with a friend, and they were talking about prayer. The friend claimed he was never distracted in prayer, so the saint made a bet: "Say an entire Our Father without getting distracted, and I will give you my horse."

The man began, "Our Father, who art in … If I win the bet, can I have your saddle too?"

This shows that, far from being a man who did not know what the floor of his chapel looked like, St. Bernard was given to distractions in prayer, just like all of us. And yet *he is a saint.* You, too, can be a saint. You just have to persevere, to not *give in* to those distractions but work to *conquer* them, no matter how many setbacks you encounter.

My point in relating all of this is that I have endeavored not to give you a collection of stories about saints that will leave you thinking, "I can never be that perfect. I will never be a saint." Rather my goal is to inspire. Now, finding source materials on any saint that was distracted in prayer, grew angry or frustrated, was disobedient, didn't get along well with a spouse, or struggled with temptation is as hard as finding, well, a saint. Hopefully, however, each story will have something from which you *can* take inspiration to become a saint yourself, which after all is the point of such stories.

My hope is that you will come to know and emulate these older brothers and sisters in Christ, gaining them as your new heroes and, more importantly, helping you know Christ and desire a deep and intimate relationship with him. These extraordinary men and women certainly knew him. They soaked themselves in Jesus, and you will see the powerful results in the pages that follow.

Blessed Mother Teresa of Kolkata
   August 26, 1910–September 5, 1997
   Beatified October 19, 2003

Blessed Mother Mariam Thresia Chiramel Mankidiyan
   April 26, 1876–June 8, 1926
   Beatified April 9, 2000

No woman in modern times has left a mark quite like that of Bl. Mother Teresa of Kolkata (that is, Calcutta). And she left this mark in the most unassuming ways: tending a dying man, caressing and cooing to sleep an orphaned baby, and praying before the Blessed Sacrament. She did simple things that had an extraordinary impact.

Agnes Gonxha Bojaxhiu was born in what is now Macedonia. Her mother weaned her on the stories of missionaries. These tales inflamed her imagination, and at the age of twelve, she decided to follow in their footsteps and devote her life to God. She later joined the Sisters of Loreto, a missionary order, and took the name Teresa. When her superiors sent her to Kolkata, India, in 1931 to teach high school to mostly middle-class girls, it must have sent her heart racing.

But over time the festering poverty Sr. Teresa saw in Calcutta began to gnaw at her. Even the most impoverished parts of the

United States, Britain, and Canada don't compare to the destitution found in places such as India. And while we may experience this for a week or two as tourists in a third-world country, Sr. Teresa saw it every day, walking to and from work, in the market, everywhere. She later reported how, riding a train in 1946 to Darjeeling for a retreat, she literally heard God call her to do something about it. Obtaining permission in 1948 to leave her order, she decided to devote herself to helping the poor wherever she found them. Sr. Teresa had no funds, no hospice, no food kitchen, no helpers, nothing but her trust in God.

But this trust, this *faith*, accomplished much. She taught the illiterate to read. She cared for those who had been left to die. She provided a home to those who had none. She gave a warm heart to children who would have otherwise known no love at all.

All of this was animated by her love for Jesus. Indeed, Sr. Teresa called the poor and sick "Christ in a distressing disguise." This passionate devotion to Christ in those of humble circumstances came out of her devotion to him in his most humble appearance of all, that of a mere piece of bread. She required her Missionaries of Charity to attend daily Mass and to do one holy hour each day in the presence of the Blessed Sacrament.

By now it is well-known that Mother Teresa had mystical, ecstatic experiences of our Lord during her early years in India, and that these abruptly ended around the time she left the Sisters of Loreto. For decades she experienced profound doubts, feelings of abandonment, and discouragement over her efforts and even her prayers. But as Professor Carol Zaleski has written, "What made her…work possible was not a subjective experience of ecstasy but an objective relationship to God," even if there was nothing to sense that relationship.

[She turned] her feeling of abandonment by God into an act of abandonment to God. It would be her Gethsemane, she came to believe, and her participation in the thirst Jesus suffered on the Cross. And it gave her access to the deepest poverty of the modern world: the poverty of meaninglessness and loneliness. To endure this trial of faith would be to bear witness to the fidelity for which the world is starving. "Keep smiling," Mother Teresa used to tell her community and guests, and somehow, coming from her, it doesn't seem trite. For when she kept smiling during her night of faith, it was not a cover-up but a manifestation of her loving resolve to be "an apostle of joy."[1]

It is hard to argue with the results. By 2007 Mother Teresa's order was in 120 countries; had 5,000 nuns, 450 brothers, and over a million coworkers; and operated 600 missions, schools, and orphanages. The number of marginalized persons her successors serve is innumerable.

Perhaps her greatest legacy, however, is the impact she made on the millions she inspired to follow her example and the souls that were saved in the process.

But Mother Teresa wasn't the first of her kind in India. She had a forerunner, a woman named Mother Mariam Thresia Chiramel Mankidiyan, of Kerala, India.

Thresia came from a once-prominent family that had slowly sunk into poverty. Her father and brother reacted by turning to drink, her mother and she by turning to God. At age four Thresia experienced a mystical vision of Our Lady, in which she believed the Blessed Virgin told her to add "Mariam" to her name. By age eight she was fasting and was praying the rosary several times each day, and at age ten she consecrated herself to Christ. When she was twelve she began caring for the untouchables and sick, nursing the poor, and mothering orphans. With the order she later founded, this would be her life's work.

While Mother Mariam was like Mother Teresa in her care for the poor, she was like Padre Pio in that the devil attacked her, and she was like St. Rita in that she bore the stigmata. Like St. Joseph of Cupertino, she levitated. Like St. Teresa of Avila, she had ecstasies. Like St. Catherine of Siena, she had mystical visions of the Holy Family. Ironically, because of these experiences her bishop subjected Mother Mariam to exorcisms, suspecting that she was really the devil's plaything. She humbly submitted and was eventually exonerated; her exorcist even became her spiritual director.

Mother Mariam died in 1926 from an infected leg wound, and both miracles attributed to her have to do with healing legs. Today her Congregation of the Holy Family has 1,584 professed sisters and 119 novices, serving in four countries, with 176 houses.

PRAYER

Dear Lord, you sent Mother Teresa and Mother Mariam Thresia to minister to the impoverished, but poverty takes different forms. There is the material poverty that afflicts much of the world, and then there is the spiritual poverty, the poverty of meaning, and the poverty of companionship that afflicts so many of us in the prosperous, developed world. You may never ask us to go to the streets of Kolkata or Mumbai, but you place in our paths those treated like lepers. Through your grace, we encounter oceans of the spiritually destitute, and we come to know in a familiar way their quest for meaning. Help us to minister your love to these people, and through the prayers of both these Mothers, help us to worry not so much about being successful for you but about being faithful to you.

Blessed Jakob Gapp

July 26, 1897–August 13, 1943

Beatified November 24, 1996, Feast of Christ the King

In 1920 Brother Josef Wagner, s.m., arrived at the train station to pick up a new candidate for the Society of Mary's novitiate at Greisinghof, Austria.

A gaunt, twenty-three-year-old Austrian World War I veteran and former prisoner of war named Jakob Gapp stepped forward, held out his hand, and introduced himself by declaring, "Here I am. I am a socialist, and I would like to become a priest. If that is not possible, please tell me so right away, and I will go home."[1] Keep in mind that socialists in Europe at this time were almost unfailingly atheists.

Even if Jakob Gapp was a Christian, it is not certain he really wanted to be a priest. His niece reported, "Jakob definitely wanted to study, but there was no money for him to do so. He happened to get a brochure in which the Society of Mary offered young men educational opportunities. Jakob claimed this possibility for himself."[2] As Fr. Gapp wrote before professing perpetual vows, "My reasons for entering were by no means free of selfishness and worldly motives."[3]

Whatever his motives for entering the Marianists, by the time he presented himself for ordination in 1930, he had become a fully convinced Catholic. So much so that his superiors made him a teacher of religion in several Marianist schools and even a director of religious education. He also served several people as their spiritual director and had an apostolate of service and care for the poor.

By 1938 the Nazis were firmly in power in Austria, and the fact that Fr. Gapp had a predilection for preaching that Jews were children of God—and that it was unchristian to treat them as anything less—had the Gestapo watching him. He also proclaimed that no Nazi could be a true Christian and no true Christian a Nazi.

Perhaps the last straw came when he spoke of how Nazism was both repulsive and totally irreconcilable with the Catholic faith. This fearless stance embarrassed and frightened his confreres, who did not appreciate his rocking the boat. Recall that at the time the Nazi leadership was beside itself over some Christian leaders' consistent witness against the regime's policies and had decided to make an example of troublesome priests. Thus Gapp's superiors advised him to leave the country.

First he went to France, where he again taught in schools, and then to Spain. It was there, in November 1942, that he was lured over the French border by two "Jews" to whom he was providing religious instruction. He fell for the ruse, and the Gestapo arrested him.

The Nazis brought Fr. Gapp to Berlin, where they tortured and interrogated him, and transcripts of those interrogations show he fearlessly proclaimed the gospel. On reading them, S.S. head Heinrich Himmler reportedly observed that if the Nazis had as much commitment to their cause as Fr. Gapp had to Jesus and the Catholic faith, Germany would easily win the war.

In letters to loved ones written hours before his execution, Fr. Gapp wrote of his faith in God's mercy. He advised his family not to be sad, since he would be with our Lord in paradise. He was guillotined on August 13, 1943, exactly twenty-three years after this former socialist met Brother Wagner at the train station.

PRAYER

God, you can write straight with crooked lines. To think you took a probable atheist and turned him into a staunch disciple who loved you so much, he died rather than deny you. Through his example and prayers, help us to love you just as much, and may that love bear fruit for your kingdom.

Blessed Ignatius Maloyan

April 11, 1869–June 11, 1915
Beatified October 7, 2001

Another twentieth-century martyr was Bishop Ignatius Maloyan. This Armenian-rite Catholic priest lost his life in the Armenian genocide at the hands of the Turks.

Ordained a priest in 1896, Fr. Maloyan was first stationed in Egypt. He eventually came back to his native land, where in 1911 he was elected bishop. Because of his predecessor's laxity, his see was in a terrible mess, and Maloyan was tasked with straightening things out. He dedicated his efforts to the Sacred Heart, to which he had a profound devotion.

By this time the Ottoman Empire's government was enacting greater and greater restrictions on his countrymen. If you were a Christian Armenian, you couldn't serve in the army, you couldn't be a policeman, you couldn't hold a government job. Further, you had to turn in any firearms or risk death.

Things came to a head during Holy Week in 1915. An exquisitely sadistic police chief named Mamdouh Bey desecrated a local church, destroying altars and violating tombs on the pretext that he suspected bombs were on the premises. He later had Bishop Maloyan and another eight hundred souls arrested. In the kangaroo court that followed, he encouraged the bishop to become a Muslim. His Excellency's response was emphatic:

Muslim? There is no way I would reject my religion and my Savior. I have been brought up in the holy Catholic Church, assimilated the base of its truthful teachings from a young age and became proficient in its undisputable facts until I unworthily became one of its pastors. I consider the shed of my blood for my faith to be the sweetest thing to my heart because I know for sure that if I get tortured for the love of the One who died for me I would become one of the happiest blessed people, and I will see my Lord and my God in heaven. You can only beat me and cut me into pieces, but I will never deny my religion.[1]

This statement incensed the bishop's captors, who accused him of blaspheming their faith. They proceeded to torture him and extract his toenails. (If you think it feels bad to stub your toe, imagine this sometime.)

On the Feast of the Sacred Heart, Mamdouh ordered that 416 of the prisoners and the bishop be marched in chains into the desert. They wore only the sweat produced by the intense summer heat. Mamdouh had each of the 416 men shot. It was as if he were trying to make Maloyan a modern-day King Zedekiah, whose sons were slain one by one before his eyes (see 2 Kings 25:7).

Before giving the bishop his turn, Mamdouh asked, "Will you not now declare publicly that you will become a Muslim?"

"I am surprised to hear you repeat the question," Maloyan retorted. "I have told you many times already that I live and die for my faith, the true faith, and that I glory only in the Cross of my sweet Savior."[2]

Mamdouh then shot him point-blank, and as Maloyan's body crumpled to the ground, he was heard to say, "My God, have mercy on me. Into Your hands I commend my spirit."[3]

PRAYER

Lord, how little we appreciate the precious faith you have bequeathed to us by grace. Most of us in the West have never had to suffer for our profession of Jesus Christ. Indeed, we take belief in you and the freedom to worship you for granted. Through the example of Bl. Ignatius and so many other martyrs, help us to remember the pearl of great price your death on the cross has won for us, and help us to always be true to you.

Blessed Alberto Marvelli

March 21, 1918–October 5, 1946

Beatified September 5, 2004

5

Many have heard of Bl. Pier Giorgio Frassati, the dashing and handsome young man who died in the mid-1920s after doing so much to spread the gospel. One who took Bl. Pier Giorgio as his inspiration, serving the poor and accomplishing extraordinary things for Christ, was another young Italian named Alberto Marvelli.

The second of seven boys born to a homemaker and a banker, Alberto lived in an impoverished area on the eastern shore of northern Italy, among struggling fishermen and masons and many unemployed people. To help alleviate the attendant poverty, his parents made their home into a center of charity and in this way taught Alberto to always take a personal role in helping others with their needs. He especially learned this from his mother, a lay tertiary for the Sisters of Charity. There were times when she would take Alberto's dinner plate, scrape half its contents onto another, and hand that to a pauper at their door. If he complained she would shrug and say, "Jesus has come, and he is hungry."[1]

In similar ways large and small, Alberto's parents taught him a profound love of the faith and a dedication to the gospel, virtues that likewise were nurtured at the local Salesian Oratory. The Salesians also stoked his love of sports, especially biking. Later his bike became the vehicle that allowed him to carry out the great works of charity and the lay apostolate for which he became known.

From the time he was a teen, Alberto would spend a half hour per day in meditation and spiritual reading. Additionally he prayed both the rosary and the Angelus daily and frequently attended Mass, in addition to confessing each week. All of this we know from the spiritual diary he began keeping at age fifteen.

"What a new world opens up to me contemplating Jesus in the Blessed Sacrament," he wrote. "Each time I receive Holy Communion, each time Jesus in his divinity and humanity enters into me, in contact with my soul, it awakens holy ideas in me, a burning and consuming flame, but one that makes me so happy!"[2]

Now, Alberto was no "add water and stir" saint. According to his friend and the vice postulator of his cause, Don Fausto Lanfranchi, he struggled daily with his faults. Father says Alberto wrote,

> How many times at the foot of the altar have I promised to become purer and more sincere, but just as many times, I have failed. Lord, help me to vanquish my quick-trigger impatience, to contain my often unhealthy curiosity and my inordinately unbridled imagination, my readiness to speak badly of others, and pull down the walls of my pride and haughtiness.[3]

Still he understood what it took to become a saint: "For us to proceed in the spiritual life, our efforts must be constant and determined. We need to continuously progress step by step, day by day, minute by minute, always aspiring to that which is our highest summit: God."[4]

Alberto attended the University of Bologna, where he graduated with an engineering degree. Although World War II was raging, he didn't have to enlist because his two brothers were already serving, and Italian law limited the number of sons who could serve in combat at any one time. He went to work at the local Fiat auto plant for a period. Eventually he left to teach high school, hoping to have a positive influence on those in an otherwise entirely secular environment.

In his spare time Alberto devoted himself to prayer and helping the poor, and the latter became especially important as the war increasingly impacted the disadvantaged. He used his salary to buy blankets and food for the needy, and after air raids he was often seen riding his bike to bring these goods to those devastated by the blasts as well as to comfort the dying. He would give people his shoes or even his bike. During the German occupation he risked his life to break open railway cars full of people destined for concentration camps.

Because of his obvious concern for the common good, his town of Rimini placed Alberto in charge of civil engineering after the war. This put him in a position to help the needy by allocating housing for them. He opened a soup kitchen and would invite the beneficiaries to Mass. He was frequently heard to say, "The poor are on our doorstep; the others can wait."[5]

Alberto did so well in his endeavors he was made a city councilman. Indeed, he eagerly entered politics because he recognized the threat posed by the communists in postwar Italy and understood the destructive effect of their atheistic ideology on people's souls. What is remarkable is that he was so well respected, even some communists supported him. One of his Marxist opponents said, "I don't mind if my party loses, so long as the engineer Marvelli becomes mayor."[6]

One night Alberto was cycling to an evening elections meeting on a poorly lit road when a speeding army truck came around a corner and hit him. He never regained consciousness. He had just sent a letter to a woman he was dating, asking her to marry him.

PRAYER

Father, for all his twenty-eight years, Alberto Marvelli dedicated himself to becoming holy. As Pope John Paul II noted during his beatification ceremony, his life is a call for all of us to find our path to sanctity in our family, in our community, in our politics, and in our profession. Help us to find this path, Lord. Give us the graces necessary to mirror his example in our own lives.

Blessed Eurosia "Mamma Rosa" Fabris

September 27, 1866–January 8, 1932

Beatified November 6, 2005

6

Have you ever thought, "This is how I want things to go," only to have God effectively tap you on the shoulder and say, "Um, I have different plans"? Welcome to the world of Eurosia Fabris.

A real-life George Bailey (from the movie *It's a Wonderful Life*), Eurosia grew up in Marola, near Vicenza, Italy. This country hamlet was the sort of small town we tend to idealize, a place where everyone knew everyone and where people helped each other in times of need. Few if any were wealthy.

As a child Eurosia could only attend school for a short while, for her family needed her to work. In her two years of schooling, however, she learned enough to read her catechism, works of the saints such as Francis de Sales, and, most importantly, the Bible, truly the font of her wisdom. This habitual reading helped foster her lifelong, total devotion to God's will. Her only desire was to follow Christ absolutely, which she thought would mean entering a convent.

But while Eurosia was fervent, she was also humble. Each day she prayed to grow in her faithfulness and docility to the will of her Beloved so as to generously respond to whatever he wanted.

And so it was when her neighbor Carlo Barban left town to care for a sick relative in a distant town. While Carlo was away his wife and one of his three daughters died, leaving two girls—both under the age of four—without anyone to care for them. Eurosia became their caretaker for the next half year.

Now, it wasn't simply her town's culture or values that prompted Eurosia to give of herself so generously. Rather, the biggest influence was her love of Jesus. For her, Jesus was everything.

Shortly after Carlo's homecoming, God showed Eurosia what his will was. Her pastor and relatives told her, "Rosa, we understand you want to be a sister, but this man needs a wife, and these girls need a mother." Eurosia placed all her trust in Divine Providence and agreed to this proposal.

In addition to her two stepdaughters, Eurosia and her husband had nine children. By all accounts it was a good marriage. She was Carlo's wife not simply out of duty to God's will; rather she loved him and he her. It is often noted how he came to value her as his "confidant and adviser."[1]

Carlo was a good provider, but the family often struggled to make ends meet, and Rosa had to find creative ways to stretch the budget. Nonetheless she realized that there were those who were worse off, and so she helped the poor however she could.

At no time was this truer than during World War I. Rosa was in her early fifties at this point, most of her children were grown, and yet she didn't hesitate to bring orphaned children into her home.

Another distinguishing feature of Eurosia was her joyful attitude toward life. While she undoubtedly grew frustrated over the hardships that beset her, she really worked and generally succeeded at looking at everything with a simple, humble, and joyous heart. Her attitude grew out of her being a Franciscan tertiary, which taught her "poverty and self-denying labor in the cause of Christ."[2]

Eurosia's positive outlook likely was a decisive influence on three of her sons, who became priests. Someone asked her, "Aren't you sad to lose three of your sons to the priesthood?" (Keep in mind that at the time, sons were often seen as an economic necessity, as well as one's source of care in old age.) "The boys we send to the Lord are like a treasure," she responded. "We have confidence in God that He will never allow us to lack for life's necessities. The sons the Lord has given to us, they are His before they are ours. And if He wants them for Himself, we must be grateful, indeed happy, for this is a great honor."[3]

Carlo died in 1930, and Eurosia followed him two years later. Her cause for canonization was taken up in 1975, and she was beatified in Vicenza's cathedral on November 6, 2005. Many of her children, grandchildren, great-grandchildren, and great-great-grandchildren were present. The cathedral could not accommodate the large crowd, so even some of her family had to watch the Mass on video monitors in an overflow room.

PRAYER

Holy Trinity, we thank you for having enriched your servant Eurosia with many treasures of grace, faith, and charity. These rendered her a charming model of domestic virtues, especially for young people, spouses, and mothers. We ask that you, who have exalted the humble and simple of heart in heaven, consent to glorify here on earth for our example and comfort the simple and humble "Mamma Rosa," and grant us the grace we ardently ask of you. Through her intercession bless our family, so that we may become a sweet sanctuary of virtue, love, and peace. Amen.

Three Glory Bes with the invocation "Holy Trinity, one God, have mercy on us!"

Blessed Vicente Vilar David
June 28, 1889–February 14, 1937

Beatified October 1, 1995

7

Valentine's Day. It calls to mind visions of romance and the hope of unquenchable love between soul mates. Imagine then that you are married to the person of your dreams. Imagine it is Valentine's Day. And then imagine you are saying good-bye to one another, just as you have throughout your marriage, except that this occasion is different. On this day, instead of knowing with reasonable certainty that you will return home, you are reasonably certain this is the last time you will lay eyes on one another in this life.

So it was with Vicente Vilar David.

Born in 1889 in the small town of Manises in the province of Valencia, Spain, Vicente was a man of remarkable intelligence, excelling in physics, chemistry, and calculus. He wanted to become a civil engineer and build bridges and roads. His father, however, prevailed on him to join the family ceramics business, and so he became an industrial engineer instead. There is no record of his feelings over this change in plans, but we can imagine how difficult it must have been to give up his dreams.

When his father died, Vincente and his three brothers began to run the business. Because of his talents his brothers made him technical director, but he did much more. He strove to improve the quality of life of his workers by implementing, among other improvements, sick pay and pensions. The workers loved him for treating them as his equals. He even founded a school of ceramics in Manises, to help train others for the trade and to help Spain compete internationally. As a result of these and other accomplishments, he was appointed deputy mayor and got to help inaugurate Valencia's airport.

But Vicente's greatest accomplishment was helping others to know Jesus. He would arrange for priests to say Mass at the ceramics plant so that his men could receive the Eucharist more regularly. He was a children's catechist and served the poor, especially during Spain's terrible civil war, which pitted the Republicans (that is, communists) against the Nationalists. Indeed, in all the stories about him, the one thing that is noted most often is how committed he was to spreading the gospel through his good works. When the communists came to power in 1931, he even risked his life to hide nuns and priests in his home so they could continue ministering to the people.

Since Valencia was in communist territory during the civil war, Vicente's unabashed Catholicism made him a marked man. This was despite the fact that he gave assistance wherever it was needed, whether to Nationalist or Republican. He even gave freezing Republican soldiers blankets and shoes from his house.

The communists made him resign as teacher and secretary at the ceramics school he had founded. Next they seized his factory, and he became an ordinary worker there. Then they arrested him, although his only crime was being a good Christian. In a regime where persecution of the Church was supposed to cow people into rejecting their holy faith, his boldness in supporting it was a problem.

And so it was that on Valentine's Day 1937, a tribunal summoned Vicente and ordered that he stop his activities on behalf of Christ and his Church. Vicente refused. The officials threatened him with the loss of everything dear to him. He stood his ground. They threatened him again, this time more harshly. He said he would rather die than renounce his faith.

Fine, the tribunal told Vicente; have it your way. Partly because of his standing in the community, they allowed him to return home to see his wife of just over fourteen years one last time.

The lovers kissed and said good-bye. As Vicente left, Isabel called after him, "See you tomorrow!" to which he replied, "Tomorrow or in heaven!"[1]

Vicente's last words, however, were words of forgiveness spoken to his captors after they had dragged him a few blocks and before they shot him. It is said that Isabel heard the gunshot. Did she know that shot had taken her husband's life? How could she not have?

For three days after Vicente's death, this holy businessman's bereaved employees went on strike. When ordered back to work by the authorities, the men told them where to go. "You haven't just taken our boss," they said, "you have taken our father." [2]

PRAYER

Dear God, how often we are tempted to push you into the background because we're afraid of standing out in a crowd, afraid of how it will look. And yet what opportunities to bring people to you could be had if only we would be bold. Help us, heavenly Father, to follow Bl. Vicente's example by doing all for you, by putting you first and our own prideful sense of self last.

Saint Jan Sarkander

December 20, 1576–March 17, 1620

Beatified May 6, 1860

Canonized May 21, 1995

8

Imagine a darkened church illumined only by the candles burning before statues up and down the nave and the sun shimmering through stained-glass windows. Above the confessional a green light is on. You slip in and recite the familiar words, "Bless me, Father, for I have sinned. It has been two weeks since my last confession. In that time …"

And thus you begin to pour your heart out, divulging your innermost secrets, your sins.

The only reason that *any* of us do this is because we know that Father will never divulge what we tell him. Indeed, he would probably sooner accept death. And so we have the context of this tale of Fr. Jan Sarkander, martyr for the seal of the confessional.

As a boy Jan studied with the Jesuits to be a priest, but for some reason he abandoned his studies and married. After his wife died following just a year of marriage, he reentered the seminary and ultimately received holy orders. He was stationed in the predominantly Protestant town of Olomouc in the Czech province of Moravia.

At this time tensions between Protestants and Catholics were incredibly high, and this was especially true in areas such as

Olomouc. The town's most prominent resident was the influential and fiercely Catholic Baron Ladislaus of Lobkowitz, whose goal was to return the area to Catholicism. Father Sarkander's excellent pastoral sensibilities helped this effort: The young priest brought 250 Protestants back to the faith of their ancestors. Unfortunately, this earned him the hatred of a local Lutheran landowner named Bitowsky von Bystritz.

By 1618 the religious tensions in the area had reached a boiling point, culminating in the outbreak of the Thirty Years' War. Protestants eventually gained control of Moravia. Determined to erase the Church from the land, von Bystritz forced Fr. Sarkander into exile.

But after a pilgrimage to the Shrine of Our Lady of Czestochowa, Father realized that his flock needed a shepherd, and so he returned to Olomouc. When marauding Poles and Cossacks invaded Moravia and approached the town to pillage it, Fr. Sarkander vested himself and processed with the Eucharist held aloft in a monstrance. He came before the Catholic forces, who to a man dropped to their knees in adoration of our Lord in the Blessed Sacrament. Father blessed the army before him, which then quietly turned and left.

When he returned to town, however, von Bystritz accused him of being a spy and had him arrested for treason. He stated that the priest had helped plan the invasion while in exile. To make him confess to this, von Bystritz had Fr. Sarkander subjected to cruel tortures. But the tortures to make him divulge what Baron Lobkowitz had said in the confessional were even crueler. Surely, von Bystritz's accomplices said, Lobkowitz had initiated the assault and had divulged his plans to Father.

The men burned the priest all over his body. At one point they coated him with oil, pitch, sulfur, and feathers to make him more flammable. They stretched him on the rack. Still he refused to violate the seal of the confessional. After a month of this treatment he finally died.

PRAYER

Heavenly Father, we thank you for the gift of the sacrament of reconciliation, where the redemption Jesus Christ won on the cross is applied to our personal sins. We further praise you for priests such as Jan Sarkander who keep inviolate that sacrament's seal, even at the cost of their lives. Make us worthy of these great gifts and your mercy, which they represent.

Blessed Laura Vicuña

April 5, 1891–January 22, 1904

Beatified September 3, 1988

9

Many know the story of St. Maria Goretti, the young Italian girl who died defending her virginity. What many don't know is that a number of other young girls such as Laura Vicuña died as martyrs for chastity. They serve as a timely inspiration for the many who suffer from abuse and sexual assault today.

Laura's tale is not the typical "martyr for chastity" narrative. There wasn't one single act in which someone tried to take her virginity and her refusal cost her her life. Rather she had to rebuff repeated assaults before coming to her end at the hands of an abuser.

Laura's life was a sad one from the start. Born into a prominent Chilean political family, her father died in a civil war. Fearing for the lives of Laura and another daughter then growing within her womb, Laura's mother, Mercedes, fled over the border to Las Lajas, Argentina. There she eventually gave birth. Broke, homeless, and with two young daughters to support, she was in desperate straits.

A beautiful woman, Mercedes attracted the attention of Mañuel Mora, a wealthy landowner for whom she worked. He made her an offer: Continue to struggle to provide for your daughters, or live with me as my mistress. Desperate and not knowing what else to do, Mercedes consented to live with him.

If there was a benefit to this tragic situation, it was that Mora paid for the girls to board at the local school run by Salesian women religious. Here, inspired by the goodness and holiness of both the sisters and the community's priests, Laura thrived and became both a good student and an exceptionally pious little girl. In fact, her evident piety bothered her classmates. When the local bishop visited, she was probably the only student who told him she wanted to be a nun.

Laura was eleven years old at the time but was already beginning to look like a young woman. When she came home on holiday, the lecherous Mora began to make advances. As time went on Laura had to spend more and more time devising ways to avoid him. At a party one night, Mora asked her to dance, and her refusal infuriated him. Finally, with his lust thwarted and ego bruised, he cut off funding for her education.

Luckily the Salesian sisters stepped in and obtained a scholarship for Laura. And finally understanding her mother's predicament, Laura gained her confessor's consent to offer her life as a sacrifice for Mercedes's return to the Church.

Not long afterward the girl became gravely ill and returned home. Despite her weakened and vulnerable state, Mora evidently abandoned any attraction he had for Mercedes and lusted after Laura only. Thankfully, Mercedes had the courage to finally say, "Enough," and move with her daughters out of the house.

In early 1904 Mora, drunk with both alcohol and passion, ran to the family's new home. He loudly and angrily demanded that they return with him. Laura refused and ran from the house. Mora chased her. Catching her from behind, he furiously beat her in the street until she fainted. She died from her injuries a week later.

In the end Laura's prayers were answered. The very night her daughter died, Mercedes went to a nearby chapel and made her confession. She eventually married a good man, and she died in the graces of the Church.

PRAYER

Heavenly Father, comfort and console all who suffer from sexual assault and other forms of abuse. Through the prayers of Blessed Laura, help them to resist their abusers, find the help they need, and remain strong in spirit. We also pray for the soul of Mañuel Mora, and we ask that you convert the hearts of all those who torment others.

Blessed Louis and Zélie Martin

August 22, 1823–July 29, 1894, and
December 23, 1831–August 28, 1877
Beatified October 19, 2008

10

11

Pope St. Pius X called St. Thérèse of Lisieux the "greatest saint of modern times," and while this is undoubtedly true, her holiness did not just happen. If you read her autobiography, *The Story of a Soul*, you see the profound impact her parents had on all their children. Indeed, they created the atmosphere in which saints were raised. All their children who survived infancy entered the religious life.

Louis Martin was what we would today call an army brat: His father was a military officer. Louis seems to have been born with a highly developed religious sense. Indeed, at his baptism the archbishop of Bordeaux blessed the baby and told his parents, "Congratulations! That child is a predestined one."[1]

As he grew into a young man, Louis's love for God grew as well, and he subsequently developed a desire to enter religious life. The order he initially wanted to join rejected him because he knew next to no Latin. Undeterred, Louis set about learning this beautiful language. Illness then derailed his studies, and Louis discerned that God wanted him to do something else. As a result he finished a watchmaking apprenticeship he had interrupted and returned to his parents' home in Alençon a master watch-maker.

By November 1850 Louis had opened his own store and was doing so well that he added a jeweler's shop. He bought a large home and had his parents move in with him. For his leisure he would go fishing, and when he caught a really big one, he would give it to the local Poor Clares for their supper.

For eight years Louis lived an idyllic bachelor's life—working, fishing, doing charitable work, and praying. Truth be told, he was quite content, much to his mother's consternation.

Zélie Guerin was born in a village near Alençon, into a strict and joyless household. Her dad showed some kindness to her, but her mother showed no affection at all and would not even allow her and her sister to have dolls. Zélie later wrote that her childhood was "as sad as a winding-sheet."[2] She also had frequent headaches and otherwise poor health, and though she greatly desired to enter religious life, this tendency toward illness caused the Sisters of Charity to reject her candidacy, which broke her heart.

With the possibility of religious life closed, Zélie decided to marry. She had no dowry for marriage, so she asked Our Lady to help her discern how to earn one. On December 8, 1851, the Feast of the Immaculate Conception, an interior voice told her, "Make Alençon point lace."[3] She underwent training for this, after which she went into business for herself. Even though lace making was a crowded industry in Alençon, her skill and ingenuity set her apart, and her business gradually thrived.

One day in 1858 Louis and Zélie met as they were walking across a bridge. Zélie heard an interior voice tell her, "This is he whom I have prepared for you."[4] There is no evidence that Louis heard a similar voice, although some think the meeting may have been contrived by his anxious mother. In any event a courtship soon blossomed, and three months later, on July 13, 1858, the two were married.

The night before her wedding, Zélie paid a visit to her sister at the Visitation Convent in Le Mans. There she wept, and not only because of a bad toothache. It seems that even though Zélie recognized it was God's will that she be married, her heart still desired religious life, and she had some ambivalence about fully entering into marriage and all that it entails (the marital act, the pains of childbirth, and so on). And yet she prayed, "Lord, since, unlike my sister, I am not worthy to be Your bride, I will enter the married state in order to fulfill Your holy will. I beg of You to give me many children and let them all be consecrated to You."[5]

Louis, on the other hand, still had the ideal of religious life in his heart, marriage or no. Most observers agree that it was because of him that the couple lived celibately for their first ten months together. Under the direction of Zélie's confessor, they finally decided they should do as normal married couples do, and they proceeded to have seven girls and two boys in thirteen years. As the birth of her first child neared, Zélie carefully kept in mind her spiritual director's advice to stay "especially close to God, so that she might be a living sanctuary for the child within her."[6]

Sadly, four of the Martin children died before the age of five, and Zélie's father, whom she had brought into her home to nurse, passed shortly after the death of her second son. All of this left Zélie "numb" with grief. "I haven't a penny's worth of courage,"[7] she said. But God provides where we are lacking, and her simple faith in his love and providence sustained her.

Zélie wrote her sister-in-law,

> When I closed the eyes of my dear little children and
> buried them, I felt sorrow through and through.…
> People said to me, 'It would have been better never to
> have had them.' I couldn't stand such language. My chil-
> dren were not lost forever; life is short and full of mis-
> eries, and we shall find our little ones again up above.[8]

The couple's last child was a sickly girl born in 1873. When she
grew desperately ill at just three months of age, Zélie understandably feared the worst. "I have no hope of saving her," she wrote.
"The poor little thing suffers horribly.… It breaks your heart to see
her."[9] However, little Thérèse did survive and thrive, and she
became the apple of the family's eye.

Each morning Zélie and Louis attended the 5:30 Mass, and
they received the Eucharist more than once a week, which was
unusual for the times. By this point Louis had sold the watch
business and was his wife's partner in her successful lace-making
endeavor, taking care of the books. And he assisted her with rear-
ing their five daughters, of whom Zélie wrote, "We lived only for
them, they were all our happiness."[10]

In October 1876, just when it seemed the family had turned
the corner on tragedy, doctors diagnosed Zélie's breast cancer and
told her there was no hope. Not accepting this, she and some of
the family went to Lourdes to pray for a cure. Our Lord had other
plans, however, and he took her to him on August 28, 1877.

Louis was now left to care for his girls alone. The sale of his
watch business and now Zélie's lace shop left the family in good
financial shape. Actually, Louis was so well off that, while attending Mass at Lisieux's cathedral and hearing the priest ask for help

with the cost of a new altar, he donated the entire ten thousand francs, roughly the equivalent of twenty-eight thousand dollars today.

It was around this time that Louis revisited Alençon (the family had moved to Lisieux). Kneeling before the altar in the church where he and Zélie had married, he offered himself as a victim for the salvation of souls. As St. Paul writes in Colossians 1:24, "Now I rejoice in my sufferings for your sake, and in my flesh I complete what is lacking in Christ's afflictions for the sake of his body, that is, the Church."[11]

Already in 1887 Louis had suffered a stroke. This was followed by two minor seizures, which affected his mobility and even mental capacity. He told a doctor, "I know why God has sent me this trial. I never had any humiliation in my life; I needed one."[12]

Barely mobile and completely dependent on the care of his daughter Céline, Louis Martin passed away in the summer of 1894.

PRAYER

Dear Lord, you ordained that marriage was for the procreation and education of children, as well as to provide each spouse with a helpmate. In Louis and Zélie Martin, you have given us an example of how married couples can fulfill both purposes. Through their prayers may spouses help one another become perfected in you.

Saint Crispin of Viterbo

November 13, 1668–May 19, 1750

Beatified September 7, 1806

Canonized June 20, 1982

12

When we look around us, we easily see so many troubles and needs, and because of original sin, there always will be. Take poverty, for example. Our Lord told us, "The poor you will always have with you" (Matthew 26:11). We look around us, and we see just how true that is. It can be kind of depressing, actually. But that doesn't mean we shrug our shoulders and do nothing. We do what we can, and a great example for us in this is St. Crispin of Viterbo.

Crispin was born Peter Fioretti, and when he was just five, his very pious mother committed him to the Blessed Virgin's care. "Look," she told him, "this is also your mother. I have made you a gift to her."[1] One of his first memories, this event made an indelible impression on him, and from that point on, he called Our Lady "Mamma."

Peter's parents taught him how to live for Our Lord. Their example worked so well that, not only did he follow them in becoming a faithful Catholic, but he exceeded them. People in his hometown of Viterbo called him "the little saint."

After Peter's father died his impoverished mother could not afford his education, so his uncle provided for this and also put him to work as a cobbler's apprentice. Although Peter became very good at this trade and probably could have made a comfortable living at it, he decided at age twenty-five that he wanted to follow God and the example of his hero, St. Felix of Cantalice, by becoming a Capuchin monk. Perhaps not surprisingly, his holy mother objected at first, possibly because sons were one's support in old age. But when Peter told her he was going to be with the "Mamma" to whom she had given him, she consented.

Peter took the habit and the name Crispin. His time as a Capuchin almost came to a quick end when the novice director, observing his exceptionally thin frame and thinking him too frail, wanted to kick him out. Soon, however, Crispin showed he was tough enough to handle anything asked of him. Furthermore, while some are good at praying but not working, and others are good at working but let their spiritual life suffer, he was good at integrating both.

Crispin was also very brave. When epidemics broke out in several nearby cities, he threw himself into caring for the people, totally neglecting his own health and safety. And if he met someone experiencing a hardship—say an unwed mother or a destitute family—he did everything he could to ease the burden. He became very good at begging, because not only was he charged with providing for the Capuchin brothers' bare necessities but he also obtained provisions for his "big family," the needy whom the friars served.

Occasionally mothers would leave their babies on the friary doorstep to be raised in its orphanage. Crispin helped care for these foundlings, and when they came of age, he would arrange for their apprenticeship in some trade and stay in touch with them throughout their lives.

Each day Crispin went into the prisons and made sure the prisoners had enough food, that it was good, and that the guards were respecting the men's dignity. Most importantly, he helped lead many convicts and other sinners—prostitutes, adulterers, and usurers—to repentance.

Looking at all the misery that regularly presented itself to him, Crispin asked himself, why? For instance, what turned people to stealing? After thinking about it he realized that many of those doing bad things usually weren't bad people. Rather, many felt compelled by their desperate circumstances to take the actions they did. Similarly, those in other difficult situations were often forced into them by people who had acted unjustly toward them.

So Crispin would dispute the merchants who gouged people and who paid unjust wages. He would prevail upon them and upon lenders to forgive debts, and through gentle prodding, humor, and wisdom, he was often successful. Just as often, however, he upset the apple cart, and many people looked on him as an aggressive, opinionated busybody.

There was a nun in the town who came to especially despise Crispin. Christian charity? She gave him none but treated him with utter contempt. People asked why he put up with it. He answered, "Praise God that there is one woman in Orvieto who knows me and treats me as I deserve."[2]

Crispin's ability to alleviate other people's burdens caused him problems even in his own friary. Because he was so good at relieving want, some of his brothers thought he should make friary life a little less harsh. They didn't want to live on just the bare necessities, but that is all Crispin ever procured for them, leaving the best for the needy outside the monastery walls. Let's face it, it takes a very special grace to embrace Lady Poverty each and every day, as Franciscans are called to do (and the Capuchins are a type of Franciscan). But Crispin told the friars, "One doesn't get to heaven in a taxi."[3] You can imagine how popular this made him.

Crispin often calmed tempers by smiling and telling a joke, usually a self-deprecating one. He called himself the "ass of the Capuchins," and when asked why he went bareheaded, he responded, "An ass does not wear a hat."[4] After his transfer to Rome, Clement XI would come to the kitchen in which Crispin worked as a cook, because he made His Holiness laugh.

Crispin also had the power of healing. The pope's own doctor told him, "You're a better healer than me." "You are a wise doctor, and the city of Rome acknowledges that fact," the saint replied. "But the Holy Virgin is much wiser than you and all the physicians of the world."[5]

Once a well-heeled gentleman asked him to cure him by his prayers to St. Mary, and Crispin told him, "Sir, you want the Blessed Virgin to cure you, but tell me, he who offends the Son, does he not also grieve the Mother? True veneration of the Blessed Virgin consists in not offending her Divine Son in any way."[6] The man realized that the root of his ailment was spiritual, and amending his life, he soon got well.

On May 19, 1750, at eighty-two years of age, Crispin died of pneumonia.

PRAYER

Dear God, each day presents us with many opportunities to serve you, whether it be in providing the needy a little extra help, bringing a smile to someone who is down, gently correcting a sinner, or providing an ear and counsel. Like St. Crispin, help us to recognize the many different ways we may serve you, and help us to not let one of them go unused.

Saint Gianna Beretta Molla

October 4, 1922–April 28, 1962

Beatified April 24, 1994

Canonized May 16, 2004

13

Our age proclaims the importance of looking good, having beautiful possessions, and being financially successful. It usually ignores, however, the most important thing, the one that makes it possible to enter heaven: loving God and demonstrating that by loving others. Gianna Molla understood what was truly important and out of love dedicated her life to Someone greater than herself.

Gianna was the tenth of thirteen children. Her parents raised her with an acute religious sense, so that even as a relatively young girl, she could write in her diary of her love of Jesus: "I offer Him all my work, all my disappointments and sufferings."[1] Additionally it is acknowledged that her own beautiful vision of motherhood was strongly influenced by the humble example she learned from her mother, who also taught her the importance of maintaining her sanctity and purity. As a result Gianna would only attend what we would today call PG or G films, and she once said she preferred "to die rather than commit mortal sin."[2]

A very bright student, Gianna was accepted into a medical school in Milan. This scandalized some because, if she was really a "proper" Christian woman, shouldn't she simply get married as soon as possible? She said, "to be called to family life does not mean getting engaged at the age of 14."[3]

Gianna was definitely called to family life, however, and she spent her single years carefully and thoughtfully considering what it would mean to be a good spouse. "Now is the time to begin to prepare yourself for family life," she wrote while still a single woman. "You cannot follow this path if you do not know how to love. To love means to want to perfect yourself and your beloved, to overcome your egoism, and give yourself completely."[4]

Gianna was thirty-three when she finally met the man of her dreams, forty-three-year-old engineer Pietro Molla, whose sister had been her patient. Her future husband, too, had prepared himself for his vocation. Before meeting her he prayed to the Madonna for a "blessed mother for my children."[5]

The couple married in September 1955, and Gianna wrote her fiancé a few days before their nuptials of her vision for their marriage:

> With God's help and blessing, we will do all we can to make our new family a little cenacle where Jesus will reign over all our affections, desires, and actions.... We will be working with God in His creation; in this way we can give Him children who will love Him and serve Him.[6]

It wasn't long before the Molla family began growing. "God blessed us," she wrote. "We have three beautiful children. What a privilege. Three children. Three handfuls!"[7]

The family was a happy one by all accounts. The parents taught their brood to appreciate the outdoors by indulging in their love for skiing and hiking in the nearby mountains. Most of all, however, they made sure to teach the kids what their parents had taught them, a love for our Lord in the Eucharist and his Blessed Mother, by daily family prayer and frequent Mass attendance.

Gianna was the soul of these efforts. As her husband later said, her whole life was "a perennial action of faith and charity; it was a non-stop search for the will of God for every decision and for every work, with prayer and meditation, Holy Mass and the Eucharist."[8]

Even though she was now a mother, Gianna continued working as a doctor, not because the family needed the money but because she saw medicine as a way of being Christ in the world. Doctors, she believed, "are called to bring God into a situation where priests are not able to assist."[9] Their mission is important. "They work with priests, who are ministers of God; they work with human beings, who are created in the image of God, and they are present during the most sacred moments of life," she wrote herself. "Never forget this." She also said, "Whoever touches the body of a patient touches the body of Christ."[10]

In 1961 Gianna became pregnant with her fourth child. She and her husband agreed that she would leave the practice of medicine after this birth to devote herself to the children. During the pregnancy, however, doctors diagnosed her with cancer, and they urged her to take measures that, while possibly saving her, would also result in the death of her growing baby. Gianna refused.

The doctors did a less invasive surgery, and things looked promising. Still Gianna knew that the birth would be difficult. Before entering the delivery room on Holy Saturday 1962, she told her husband, "If you must decide between me and the child, do not hesitate: choose the child—I insist on it. Save the baby."[11] Fortunately, everything went well, and she gave birth to a healthy little girl, Giannina.

However, this was a time before effective antibiotics. A septic infection set in and quickly took hold of her weakened body, causing her immense pain. Several days after her daughter's birth, she asked, "Bring me home," for she knew she would soon die. Many years later her husband recounted her last moments.

> She asked [her sister] Virginia if she knew what it meant to die and to leave behind four children. The last gesture I saw Gianna make was when she was holding Giannina, and Gianna looked at the baby with both eyes … I don't know how to tell you. I don't know how to explain it. She was saying good-bye to the baby with her eyes. That expression really moved me.
>
> On Thursday, Virginia said to me, "Pietro, I was afraid she was going to cross over into the next world because of the pain, the pain she was suffering." Gianna said to me, very serenely as usual, "Pietro, I was already over there. Do you know what I saw?" "No, tell me," I replied. "Not now," she said. And she never did. "But you see," she continued, "over there, we were too content, too happy, too much in love, and God sent me here to suffer a little bit, because we cannot live without some suffering."

As she lay in her agony, she incessantly repeated the words, "Jesus, I love you."[12]

After Gianna's death Pietro raised their four children. Their second child, Mariolina, died just two years later. Giannina grew up to follow in her mother's medical footsteps.

Gianna Molla is not only the first woman physician but also the first married woman of the modern era to be declared a saint.

PRAYER

Lord Jesus, you told us the greatest commandment is to love. Help us to follow the example of St. Gianna by loving you so completely that we desire only your will and seek to perfect ourselves for your sake. Help us also to love all our brothers and sisters for love of you, to serve them for love of you, and if it be your holy will, to stand ready to die for them for love of you. Amen.

Blessed Elisabetta Canori Mora

November 21, 1774–February 5, 1825

Beatified April 24, 1994

14

Don't you sometimes wonder what God is thinking? You seem to be doing everything right—growing in virtue, leading a holy life, serving him by following what you prayerfully discern to be his will—and yet he allows you so many opportunities to suffer.

But Jesus himself told us that, to be his followers, we must pick up our cross daily and follow him (see Matthew 10:38; 16:24). The saints understood this. They lovingly embraced their crosses and, like Job, only sought to be faithful while they waited on God and his will. One who gave a perfect example of this is Elisabetta Canori Mora.

The Roman patrician Canori family knew something about bearing crosses, as they had lost six children by the time Elisabetta, the thirteenth of fourteen, was born. We can imagine that her parents raised her to accept God's will in good and bad, because despite all they had endured, the family was a happy one. They sent Elisabetta to be educated by the Augustinians at the Convent of St. Rita in Cascia, where she learned of the convent patron's conversion of a difficult husband. Did this help her as she faced her own troubles later in life?

In 1796, at the age of twenty-two, Elisabetta entered into a seemingly well-made marriage with a young lawyer, Cristoforo

Mora, whose father was a wealthy doctor. He was handsome, she was pretty, and they seemed to be made for one another. Indeed, the marriage was a happy one at first.

But Cristoforo quickly grew mentally unstable. He became controlling and cut off Elisabetta's visits to her family. Little by little he grew cold and indifferent. He was given to outbreaks of jealous rage against his virtuous and loving wife. He began cheating on her with a woman of lower social status and made no attempt to conceal the fact.

Now, many women would have rightly boiled over with fury at such treatment, but Elizabetta never reproved her husband. Instead she chose to use the same kindness and affectionate gentleness that had won his heart in the first place. Sadly this was to no avail.

In the first three years of her marriage, Elisabetta had some happiness in bearing three children. The last, Marianna, was a true bundle of joy. Yet there was a cross in having three young ones to care for, for Cristoforo neglected his family and his professional duties, and he made several speculative investments that were disastrous. To simply keep a roof over their heads and cover some of their debt, Elisabetta had to sell her entire jewelry collection.

You would think Cristoforo would have looked at the situation, seen how he was at fault, seen how his wife was doing heroic things for him, and come back to her with a repentant heart. You would think wrong. Instead, inflamed by his pride and humiliated by his failures, he became even worse, treating his wife with contempt, as if she was to blame for their predicament.

To help ease the young family's financial burden, Cristoforo's parents took them in, but this was additional weight on Elisabetta's cross. She was under her in-laws' constant and eventually hostile eye, with no privacy and none of the rhythms of her normal family life, however imperfect they had been. Instead of complaining, however, she again embraced the cross, offering her compounded suffering for her husband's conversion, for she knew well what Scripture says about the ineligibility of adulterers for entry into heaven.

In 1801 Elisabetta had another child, after which she became gravely ill. Thankfully, through prayers to Our Lady, she received a miraculous healing. It is supposed that she had occasionally doubted whether God had her in the palm of his hand, for after this point, with no doubts whatsoever, she became intensely fervent in her prayer life.

She began to receive Communion more than once a week, and she frequented the confessional more often. She also made three resolutions: to be unfailingly meek and never show anger, to submit to God's will and perceive all things that happened to her as God's will, and to do penance and practice mortification for her husband's conversion (see Colossians 1:24). Maybe not coincidentally, it was around this time that she began having mystical experiences.

These practices probably helped her keep her sanity, for as if she didn't have enough to worry about, her own family relentlessly pestered her to leave Cristoforo. Furthermore, her sisters-in-law openly blamed her both for their brother's financial failings and his philandering, saying, "With a different woman, Cristoforo would be different!"[1]

To compound all of this, her husband and her in-laws began pressuring her to give written consent for her husband's adultery. Can you imagine? "It is good for me to have spent two hours in prayer!" she wrote. "God gave me so much strength that I was ready to give my life rather than to offend my Lord."[2]

When Cristoforo's father died, her in-laws kicked her out. She found a place to live and obtained a job cleaning houses. Remember that Elisabetta was a patrician: Up until now she had never done a day's work, and now she was cleaning other people's toilets. Yet this change gave her and the children a peaceful home life. She was able to devote attention to them that she couldn't before.

It was at this time that she became a third order member of the Trinitarians, an order founded to ransom slaves but now involved in other good works. Elisabetta worked to relieve suffering wherever she found it, even though she herself was impoverished. Her soul cleansed by the many purifying fires she endured (see 1 Corinthians 3:15), she became something of a spiritual advisor to many.

When Elisabetta was fifty years old, she developed dropsy, the accumulation of fluid under the skin. The condition worsened to the point where she couldn't even get up. Miraculously, her illness caused Cristoforo to return, and during her final weeks, he rarely left her bedside during the day. Did she tongue-lash him for the sewer through which he had dragged her? No, she simply loved him, telling her spouse, "You will come back to God after my death; you will come back to God to give Him glory."[3]

On Elisabetta's last night on earth, Cristoforo was with his mistress. When he returned at dawn and found her dead, the weight of his sin crashed down upon him, and he wept furiously. Nine years later he fulfilled the prophecy of his wife and became a Franciscan. He died a holy death on September 8, 1845, the Feast of the Nativity of Our Lady, to whom his wife had been so devoted.

The Church does not say that spouses must or even should stay in abusive marriages. Rather we must always work for the good of our spouses, especially their ultimate good, which is their becoming holy and obtaining a home in heaven. Willing and seeking the good of the other, after all, is the mark of true love. Elisabetta Mora did this. As John Paul II noted in his beatification homily, she, "in the midst of numerous marital difficulties, showed total fidelity to the commitment undertaken by the sacrament of marriage and to the responsibilities that flow from it."[4]

PRAYER

Dear Lord, help us to follow Elisabetta's example amid the trials of marriage and family life. Help us to stay focused on you, to forgive those who sin against us, to desire the best for them, and to have hope for your triumph over sin and death.

Blessed Isidore Bakanja

Circa 1885–August 15, 1909

Beatified April 24, 1994

15

How many of us love our holy religion so much that we are willing to share it at every opportunity, regardless of the cost? The answer is probably "Not many," and this is what makes Isidore Bakanja so remarkable.

Born a pagan in what was then the colony of Belgian Congo (now the Democratic Republic of the Congo), Isidore met some Trappist missionaries while working as an assistant mason for some colonists. Upon hearing their explanation of the faith, he not only converted but fell passionately in love with his new religion. From the time of his baptism at age eighteen, he was never without a rosary in his hand, and he never missed an opportunity to share the gospel. He loved Christ so much, in fact, that he left his village, where he was the only Christian, to find fellowship with others who shared his beliefs.

Obtaining work on a Belgian rubber plantation, Isidore began to evangelize his fellow workers. This was a problem for his overseer, Van Cauter, a committed atheist who hated God's missionaries because they taught the workers about human dignity and justice, which in turn caused dissension among the natives. The plantation's head supervisor knew and liked Isidore, and he told him to be careful about teaching the faith, but to no avail.

Seeing the profound effect Isidore's catechesis was having, Van Cauter ordered him to stop wearing his scapular and spreading the gospel. "You'll have the whole village praying, and no one will work!" he said.[1] Isidore refused to obey.

One day, during a break, Van Cauter saw him praying and flew into a rage. He beat him twice, the second time landing more than a hundred lashes with an elephant whip that had a nail at the end of it. Isidore's screams were so loud that they woke Van Cauter's concubines, who were sleeping a good distance away. Van Cauter ripped the scapular from Isidore's neck and, for good measure, kicked him in the head a few times. He stopped only when he saw that the lashes had gone through to the bone. Isidore, his legs now bound in chains, was thrown into a hut and discarded like an animal.

Because an inspector named Dorpinghaus was coming to visit the plantation, Van Cauter wanted Isidore out of the way. He told him to go to a nearby village, but Isidore could not walk, so Van Cauter had him chained again. Somehow Isidore managed to escape into the nearby jungle.

When Dorpinghaus arrived, the catechist burst out of the jungle, pleading for help. The inspector later reported that Isidore's back was "torn apart by deep, festering, malodorous wounds, covered with filth, assaulted by flies. He leaned on two sticks in order to get near me—he wasn't walking; he was dragging himself."[2]

Van Cauter tried to kill Isidore, calling him an "animal," but the inspector stopped him. Mercifully, Dorpinghaus took the young man away, hoping to heal his wounds. But Isidore simply told him, "If you see my mother, or if you go to the judge, or if you meet a priest, tell them that I am dying because I am a Christian."[3]

For six months Isidore endured the agony of his wounds. Because they had been poorly treated, blood poisoning set in, and he succumbed, praying the rosary and wearing his scapular to the end. The missionaries who tended him during his last days and brought him the sacraments were edified to learn that he had already forgiven the man who had done this to him.

"The white man did not like Christians.... He did not want me to wear the scapular.... He yelled at me when I said my prayers.... I shall pray for him. When I am in heaven, I shall pray for him very much."[4]

Van Cauter was later convicted for his crimes, and he spent several years in jail.

PRAYER

Sweet Jesus, in a society that is becoming incrementally and yet unmistakably hostile to you, it increasingly difficult to spread the faith. There are many people today who hate you no less than Van Cauter ever did. Bl. Isidore endured whipping and death for you. May his prayers likewise obtain for us the courage to preach you and your gospel come what may.

Saint Josephine Bakhita

Circa 1869–February 8, 1947

Beatified May 17, 1992

Canonized October 1, 2000

16

We all know people who have had extremely rough lives and have endured terrible things. Some of these become bitter, others become reclusive and withdrawn, while still others adapt and overcome. All hope for freedom from their past. Each has a patron in Josephine Bakhita.

Born with a twin sister into a chieftain's family in Sudan's now infamous Darfur region, Bakhita was kidnapped at age nine and sold into slavery. Over the next six years, she had five different masters. These men treated her so inhumanely—administering whippings, inflicting ritual scarring, and so forth—that she eventually forgot her name. The slavers simply called her *Bakhita*, Arabic for "lucky."

The Italian diplomat Callisto Legnani eventually bought Bakhita. He treated her so kindly that she began to believe she was really *bakhita*. He later gave her to his friend Agosto Michieli, a businessman with dealings in Sudan. Michieli made her nanny to his daughter Mimmina and brought her along when he and his family returned to their home in Venice.

Around 1889 Michieli and his wife returned to Sudan on business, leaving Bakhita and Mimmina with the Canossian sisters.

While she had likely gone to Mass with the Michielis, it was at the convent that Bakhita first encountered the person of Jesus Christ and learned of his love. In him she finally comprehended the God whom she had previously "experienced in my heart without knowing who it was."[1]

"Seeing the sun, the moon, and the stars," she wrote, "I said to myself, 'Who could be the Master of these beautiful things?' And I felt a great desire to see him, to know him and to pay him homage."[2]

Now knowing "who it was," Bakhita received all three sacraments of initiation on January 9, 1890, at the hands of the patriarch of Venice. She took the baptismal name of Josefina Margarita Afortunada. The otherwise extremely reserved woman would thereafter gratefully kiss the convent's baptismal font and joyfully exclaim, "Here, I became a daughter of God!"[3] Each day with the sisters brought new revelations of the Lord's love for her, and she grew increasingly closer to him.

Eventually the Michielis returned, but Josephine had found the happiest place she had ever known and would not leave. Mrs. Michieli complained to the authorities, who said that, since slavery was illegal in Italy and had even been outlawed in Sudan before Josephine's birth, she did not have to go with them. On the vigil of the Feast of the Immaculate Conception in 1893, when she was thirty-eight years old, the court granted her freedom. Josephine stayed with the Canossian sisters and eventually became one of them.

Sent to live at the order's house in nearby Schio, Josephine took on several jobs: cook, dishwasher, sacristan, and porter, throwing herself into each one. Most people in Schio had never seen a black woman. Once a little boy licked her hand, hoping that the "chocolate" on her skin would come off. She was always very good-natured about these misunderstandings, and the people came to love her humility, simplicity, and unfailing kindness. They affectionately called her "our little brown mother."[4]

Josephine loved the children, and she especially loved to show each of them tender affection when they came to Schio's Canossian school. She told their teachers, "You teach catechism, I will stay in the chapel and pray for you that you may teach well." Simply put, she perpetually exuded a love for and gratitude to God. "Be good, love the Lord, pray for those who do not know him," she would say. "What a great grace it is to know God!"[5]

Sometime in the 1930s Josephine was encouraged to write her story, and the resulting autobiography became a best-seller. Huge crowds came to see her wherever she went to promote the book.

Toward the end of her life, Josephine became sick and experienced much pain, but she was always unfailingly kind. After a long illness, and repeating the words "Our Lady, Our Lady," she passed to her reward with a smile on her lips.

PRAYER

Dear Lord Jesus, Josephine was once a slave under human bondage, but you took away her chains. Today so many of us struggle as slaves under sin. Through her intercession, remove us from bondage by enabling us to know you, for you have promised, "You will know the truth, and the truth will make you free" (John 8:32).

Blessed Pope Pius IX

    May 13, 1792–February 7, 1878

    Beatified September 3, 2000

17

In the history of Christendom, there have been 265 popes. While many have made an impact, few have been as consequential as Pope Pius IX. Indeed, the things he did during his thirty-two-year reign, second in length only to St. Peter's, set the course of papal history for the next hundred years and still reverberate to this day.

Born Giovanni Maria Mastai-Ferretti to a petty noble family, he left his rural home for Rome to enter the papal noble guard. His chronic epilepsy forced him out of this service, but Pope Pius VII (1800–1823) thought he would make an excellent priest and encouraged him to enter the seminary. Giovanni did, and he was ordained in April 1819.

Pius then made Giovanni auditor to Chile and Peru, to help determine how those nations were functioning from an ecclesiastical perspective. This would make Giovanni the first pontiff to have travelled to the Americas. He did very well in this assignment, and this ultimately led to his appointment as bishop of Spoleto in 1827 at age thirty-five. Spoleto was in the Papal States, that large swath of Italy whose temporal leader was the pope, and the bishop effectively ran the local government.

At the time Italy was a roiling cauldron of politics. Some simply wanted the Italian peninsula united. Others wanted anarchy. Still others had bought into the theories of Voltaire and the Enlightenment and desired the abolition of all religion. Then there were those who just wanted democracy, a free press, and freedom of religion. Today we take these for granted, but in monarchist Europe they had never known such things, and so there was great agitation for them. Keep in mind, the United States Bill of Rights had passed only forty years before.

Furthermore, many opposed these developments because by them, their proponents meant freedom from religion or freedom to use the press to actively undermine people's faith in God, to cite just one problem. Understandably, this caused problems in many people's minds.

This was the situation that surrounded the new bishop at Spoleto. Shortly thereafter Mastai-Ferretti, who sympathized with the nationalist movement, pardoned some revolutionaries, which convinced many that his sympathies lay on the liberals' side.

In 1832 Pope Gregory XVI (1831–1846) promoted him to cardinal bishop of Imola, and here he made his priority improving the formation of priests. He also regularly visited prisoners in jail and enacted programs for the numerous street children of the city.

Upon Gregory's death the conclave to choose his successor took place in an atmosphere that was heavy with the threat of revolution and the age's anticlericalism, so heavy in fact that only forty-six of the sixty-two cardinal-electors attended. Supported by the liberals because they thought him sympathetic to the currents of the age, Mastai-Ferretti was elected following several ballots. He took the name Pius, after the pope who had encouraged his vocation. Showing the often brilliant touch he brought to his papacy, he chose his runner-up to be secretary of state.

Glamorous and very handsome, Pius's election thrilled the *glitterati*, the atheists, and the Protestants. The Anglicans thought he would lead the Church toward "freedom" and "progress."

Many Catholics were thrilled as well. Pius IX was smart, kind, jovial, and unpretentious, and people could tell he was earnestly pursuing a holy life. He lived like a pauper, and each day he celebrated one Mass and attended another.

As leader of the Papal States, the pope initiated the construction of railways, which his predecessor had not allowed because, for Gregory, they symbolized all that was wrong with modernity. The pope also put up streetlights around Rome. Although he was criticized for thwarting industrial development in Rome, he was praised for implementing agricultural education for farmers so they could improve their crops, which led to an increase in the production of staples such as olive oil and wine.

Actually, Pius's all-around management of the Papal States was excellent. He even wiped out the States' chronic deficits, and tax rates there were the lowest in Europe. Additionally, the pope negotiated lower tariffs with other nations to increase exports, but even with all of this, the Papal States still weren't as prosperous as the northern parts of Italy. Thus he tried to relieve the poverty with charity, which was also criticized. He improved education and created a uniform civil code in 1859, which led to the reformation of the judicial system and in turn helped reduce crime. Furthermore, he patronized the arts, ordered the reinforcement of the about-to-collapse Colosseum, financed excavations of the catacombs, and even restored Etruscan and Roman monuments outside of Rome.

Significantly, Pius abolished the requirement that Jews attend Sunday Mass and allowed them to receive Christian charity. He opened certain professions to them that had previously been closed, and he abolished the Jewish ghetto. However, after his return in 1850, he restored it again. This was due to the distrust he developed after seeing large numbers of Jewish men in the anticlerical and revolutionary movements. Personally, however, he railed against anti-Semitism and even played Good Samaritan to an old Jew left to die in the streets.

One episode from his relations with Jews still causes controversy. A Christian servant of a Jewish family baptized their boy since he was near death, but the child recovered. The law said Christians couldn't be raised by Jews, even their own parents. So the boy went to live with the pope and eventually acknowledged him as "my adoptive father."[1] He later became a priest and spoke in favor of Pius's beatification.

One can see why the intelligentsia celebrated Pius as a model ruler. The problem was that the freed revolutionaries had not changed their views just because the pope was merciful to them. A large number went back to their old ways and even rejoined paramilitary groups, many of which were quite violent. Furthermore, the pope's concessions only stoked the demand for more concessions.

In 1848 Pius selected Pellegrino Rossi as his prime minister. Even though Rossi proposed many liberal reforms, he was too conservative for the radicals, who assassinated him in broad daylight that same year. Realizing his own safety was in danger, the pope fled to Gaeta, and the revolutionaries took control of Rome, declaring a Roman Republic. When Pius excommunicated those involved, they responded by desecrating St. Peter's Basilica on

Easter Sunday. The situation in the Eternal City deteriorated into lawlessness. French troops were brought in to crush the Republic, and with their assistance His Holiness returned to Rome in 1850.

It is one thing to want revolution, it is another thing to see it firsthand. After their experience with the radicals, the people realized what a good and benevolent ruler they had in Pius. Always magnanimous, he proclaimed he had returned "as a pastor, not an avenger,"[2] but in his heart he would never again trust the Romans, who had so readily turned on him.

As one mark of this lack of trust, Pius moved his official residence from the Quirinal Palace to the Vatican, because of the better security there. He continued to make reforms in the Papal States, but they were never enough to placate the revolutionaries' appetite.

Over the next twenty years, the nationalist forces, led by Garibaldi and King Victor Emmanuel II, progressively captured each papal state until the only one left was Lazio, which contains Rome. That too fell, and on September 20, 1870, so did Rome, and the king made it the new Italian republic's capital. A practicing Catholic, His Highness offered the pope an income of 3.25 million lire per year. Pius, however, refused both this offer and to even acknowledge that the Papal States were no longer his. Indeed, in protest of the takeover, he made himself the "prisoner of the Vatican," meaning he never ventured outside of the Holy See again.

With his income now nonexistent, Pius instituted "Peter's Pence," asking Catholics around the world to send him funds. Catholics responded, and this is still one of the Holy See's primary revenue sources.

Sadly, these political machinations threaten to obscure Pope Pius IX's remarkable achievements as pontiff and his incredibly vigorous pontificate. He is most famous for calling the First Vatican Council, which defined papal infallibility, and for proclaiming the dogma of the Immaculate Conception. Furthermore, French Catholic life flourished under his directives: Five Catholic universities were founded in that country, and 160,000 priests and religious served there by the end of his reign. He recreated the British and Dutch hierarchies, which had been dormant since the Protestant Revolt. In Spain, where liberals were bent on destroying the Church, he reached a concordat with Queen Isabella II that saw most Church property and prerogatives returned. He undertook so many efforts to build up the Church in the United States and Canada that one can legitimately call him the Father of the Church in both countries.

There were also problems. Because of the pope's vigorous efforts, German Chancellor Otto von Bismarck launched the infamous *Kulturkampf*, which severely constrained the Church's ability to function. This persecution actually increased the Church's numbers and even her stature among non-Catholics. Catholics also saw their freedoms curtailed in the Austro-Hungarian Empire, Switzerland, and Russia, which controlled Catholic Poland at the time.

All in all, however, the papacy became stronger during Pius's reign than it had been in centuries. He was the first pope to use the papal bully pulpit to great effect, writing thirty-eight encyclicals.

Ironically, one of his works, the *Syllabus of Errors*, made many see him as an enemy of progress. It condemned, among other things, the liberalizing of marriage laws, the notion that Church and state ought to be totally separated, and unfettered freedom of the press. However, if seen in the context of the times and his eighteen years of personal experience with so-called liberalism, the *Syllabus* is an understandable, prudent, even brilliant document. His purpose was to draw attention to the age's tendency to make a god of reason, which led to relativism and indifference. This is a valid observation even today.

Finally, under Pius's influence the spiritual lives of the laity improved. Catholics started going on pilgrimages again, and spiritual retreats and parish missions became more prominent parts of lay and parish life. He also reformed Church discipline and removed bad priests from service. He even wrote lyrics to the popular Italian Christmas carol "From Starry Skies Descended."

For the last ten years of his life, Pius suffered from painful skin illnesses. These had the effect of making him slow, for which he made fun of himself. The summer of 1877 was very hot, which made his condition worse. He underwent agonizing medical treatments, which he handled like a martyr. Ultimately the discomfort grew so bad that he had to be carried wherever he went.

Pius died at the age of eighty-six while praying the rosary. His last words were "Guard the Church I loved so well and sacredly."[3] When his grave was opened in 2000 for the beatification process, his body was found incorrupt.

PRAYER

Dear Lord Jesus, in Pius IX you blessed your Church with an exemplary pastor who was filled with zeal for building up the Christian life in all her people. May the Holy Roman Church always be so blessed, and may she be guarded and guided through the continued intercession of he who loved the Church so well.

Blessed Marie of Jesus Crucified

January 5, 1846–August 26, 1878

Beatified November 13, 1983

18

There are often times in our lives when we clearly see the will of God. When actually doing his will comes at a cost, however, we can grow afraid of moving forward. Marie of Jesus Crucified experienced this fear and yet persevered in doing what our Lord wanted, and she thus provides an inspiring example of trusting him always.

She was born Mariam Baouardy to a poor Greek Melkite family in Ibillin, Galilee, who had seen all but one of their previous twelve children die in infancy. Before her birth her parents travelled to Bethlehem and the Church of the Nativity to beseech Our Lady for a child who would survive to adulthood, and the Virgin answered their prayers when Mariam was born on the Vigil of the Epiphany. Sadly, however, they died when she was just two years old, and she went to live with her aunt and uncle.

Mariam was a very sweet and well-intentioned child. For instance, in her uncle's orchard she once attempted to give her caged birds a bath. They drowned, and while burying them she heard a voice tell her through her tears, "This is how everything passes. If you would give me your heart, I shall always remain with you."[1]

After her uncle moved the family to Alexandria, Egypt, he betrothed Mariam at age thirteen, a common age for marriage at the time. When she learned what wifely duties entailed, she grew distraught. She stayed up all night the eve of the wedding, praying for guidance. She heard that familiar voice say again, "Everything passes." She knew then that God willed her to become a religious. The voice then told her, "Mariam, I am with you; follow the inspiration I shall give you. I will help you."[2]

The next morning, the day of her nuptials, with the guests invited and the party paid for, the bride-to-be proclaimed her refusal to marry. Enraged, her uncle beat her. He consigned her to work as a domestic in his house, ensuring that she had the lowest, dirtiest jobs possible.

Learning of Mariam's plight, a Muslim neighbor befriended her. He pretended to be sympathetic, telling her she would never receive such treatment in his religion. When she realized he was simply trying to convert her, the Holy Spirit inspired her to exclaim, "Muslim, no, never! I am a daughter of the Catholic apostolic Church, and I hope by the grace of God to persevere until death in my religion, which is the only true one."[3] Infuriated by this profession of faith, the man slit her throat and left her to die in an alleyway. It was the Feast of Our Lady's Birth.

Lying in a pool of her own blood, Mariam had a vision.

> A nun dressed in blue picked me up and stitched my throat wound. This happened in a grotto somewhere. I found myself in heaven with the Blessed Virgin, the angels and the saints. They treated me [for four weeks] with great kindness. In their company were my parents. I saw the brilliant throne of the Most Holy Trinity and Jesus Christ in His humanity. There was no sun, no

lamp, but everything was bright with light. Someone spoke to me. They said that I was a virgin, but that my book was not finished. When my wound was healed I had to leave the grotto, and the Lady took me to the Church of St. Catherine served by the Franciscan Friars. I went to confess. When I left, the Lady in Blue had disappeared.[4]

Also during this convalescence Our Lady fed Mariam some soup. When she asked for more, the Virgin told her, "That is enough, Mariam. Do not do as those who find that they never have enough. Have enough confidence in God to know that he gives you and will always give you just what you need, no matter what."[5]

Mariam left her uncle's home and went to work as a domestic for a Christian family. Then, in 1860, she went to live with the Sisters of St. Joseph, but when supernatural events began to occur, the sisters made her leave. Finally, after a series of St. Paul-like adventures, Mariam joined the Carmelites of Pau, France, taking the name Marie of Jesus Crucified.

The young nun continued to experience supernatural events, such as ecstasies, levitation, and the stigmata. During one forty-day period she fought off demonic possession. Another time the Holy Spirit compelled her to tell Pope Pius IX that seminaries did not emphasize him enough, which was why he was neglected in the Church. Basically illiterate, she nonetheless wrote gorgeous poetry. When she came out of her ecstasies, she would say, "Where there is charity, there is God also. If you think to do good for your brother, God will think of you. If you dig a hole for your brother, you will fall into it, it will be for you. But if you make heaven for your brother, it will be for you."[6]

While Bl. Marie was holy, she was far from perfect. She could show a quick temper, which seems fitting for a woman whose name in Arabic means "gunpowder." She struggled with discouragement because she wasn't very disciplined, and she found the Carmelite life difficult. As a result she occasionally fell into despair about her salvation, but for this she took to simply trusting in the mercy of God. Thus she left behind the despair and found a simple joy.

One of Sr. Marie's crosses was the testing her superiors put her through, so that the extraordinary graces she exhibited did not lead to pride. Through it all she called upon the Holy Spirit to be her aid and never relied upon her own power.

Sister Marie eventually helped found Carmels in India and in Bethlehem. While supervising the construction of the church for the convent in the latter place, even "diving into the sand and lime,"[7] she received an injury that caused gangrene to set in, which then caused her death.

PRAYER

Lord Jesus, we make Bl. Marie of Jesus Crucified's prayer our own:

> *Holy Spirit, inspire me.*
> *Love of God, consume me.*
> *Along the true road, lead me.*
> *Mary, my good mother, look down upon me.*
> *With Jesus, bless me.*
> *From all evil, all illusion, all danger, preserve me.*[8]

Saint Charbel Makhlouf
　　May 8, 1828–December 24, 1898
　　Beatified December 5, 1965
　　Canonized October 9, 1977

19

Walk into many churches in Mexico, and you will see a statue of a man sporting a white beard, clothed in a black, hooded robe, with his arms outstretched. Before the statue is an ocean of multicolored ribbons, each a votive offering in thanksgiving for favors obtained by the intercession of this saint. While it is arresting to see these rainbow-hued mounds of satin strips, it is even more surprising when you consider that this holy man, beloved by the Mexican people, was from Lebanon and has been a saint for little more than thirty years.

What is even more surprising is that there is nothing particularly special or inspiring about this man's life story. And yet this Maronite monk, whom some call the male St. Thérèse for his hidden life of outstanding holiness and devotion to the Eucharist, deserves our consideration by virtue of what God has done through him.

Born in northern Lebanon and an orphan by age three, Youssef Antoun Makhlouf was remarkably touched by grace from the beginning. Even as a young boy, he could pray for hours. At age twenty-three he entered the Our Lady of Maifouk Monastery. A year later he went to the Maronite Monastery of St. Maron in

Annaya, Lebanon, where he took the name Charbel, after a second-century Christian from Antioch who was martyred under the Roman Emperor Trajan.

Ordained a priest in Bkerky on July 23, 1859, Charbel returned to St. Maron. In early 1875 he entered the Sts. Peter and Paul Hermitage, where he lived an austere life for his twenty-three remaining years. There he kept a voluntary vow of silence, speaking only when it became absolutely necessary to do so. He ate just one vegetarian meal per day, totally foreswearing meat and fruit, and he fasted four times per year. His bed was a mattress stuffed with dead leaves, his pillow was a log, and his blanket was a goat skin.

Fr. Charbel prayed the rosary and said Mass at 11:00 AM daily. Why so late in the morning? Because he spent hours preparing for the liturgy. In fact he rose at midnight to pray before the Blessed Sacrament. For three hours of this time he recited his breviary.

Fellow hermits reported seeing Charbel levitate during prayer. It is said that when a poisonous snake threatened the life of another monk, the saint simply asked it to please go away, and it politely complied. Reportedly Charbel had the gifts of healing and prophecy as well.

While celebrating Mass on December 16, 1898, Charbel had a stroke. It was during the Offertory, and he was reciting the prayer, "Father of Truth, behold your Son, a sacrifice pleasing to you. Accept this offering of him who died for me that I may have life. Behold the offering. Accept it...." Charbel would linger for eight nights, incessantly repeating this prayer.

Christmas Eve marked the end of Charbel's life. Not long after his burial, multicolored lights began flitting around his grave.

Some of his disciples disinterred his body and found it sweating blood and water.

As you can imagine, throngs of pilgrims flocked to Charbel's tomb, imploring his intercession. After his prayers obtained 350 miracles during a four-month period in 1950, his tomb was opened again. Although floating in mud, Charbel's corpse was found to be incorrupt and exuding a bloodlike liquid that healed the crippled and the sick when applied to them. Seeing this, many people were converted to Catholicism.

PRAYER

Dear Lord, St. Charbel led a hidden life that was totally dedicated to you. Now, through his intercession, enable us to see the power of humility and the fruits of becoming small for your glory. May we follow in his footsteps.

Blessed Marie-Joseph Cassant

March 6, 1878–June 17, 1903

Beatified October 3, 2004

20

Have you ever felt like giving up on something because, no matter how hard you try, things never seem to get any better? If so you have a friend in Bl. Marie-Joseph Cassant.

The second child of a prosperous family of orchard tenders, Joseph would play "Mass" as a little boy, and it was this experience, coupled with the fact that his parents were good catechists, that made him want to be a priest. While no one doubted the frail boy had a vocation, they did doubt whether he could ever fulfill it. Joseph had a terrible memory, and the only reason he had passing grades in school was because he worked so hard. As he would say, "Great labor overcomes all things."[1]

To help Joseph qualify for entry into the seminary, his parish priest personally instructed him in French and Latin for several months. Joseph worked like mad to learn, but that wasn't enough. His learning difficulties persisted, and the pastor reluctantly deduced that Joseph would never be able to meet the requirements of being a parish priest. Father directed his young friend to the Trappist Monastery of St. Mary of the Desert, where the training for the priesthood was less rigorous since the clerics there had no pastoral ministry.

Joseph followed his pastor's advice and entered the monastery, taking the name Marie-Joseph. Realizing what a special soul Joseph was, his novice master, Fr. André, told him after his first interview, "Only trust, and I will help you to love Jesus!"[2]

Marie-Joseph never disputed orders, nor did he openly complain, despite the fact that some friars were unkind to him because of his learning disability. This was especially true of one of his teachers. This monk grew so frustrated with Joseph's slowness and difficulty in learning his lessons that he once screamed at him, "You are totally limited! It is useless for you to study. You will not learn any more. To ordain you would be a dishonor to the priesthood."[3]

Marie-Joseph knew his weaknesses, and so he did not argue with those who criticized him. Still, he had a very sensitive soul, which many would describe as innocent like a child's. Thus this treatment made him feel very bad about himself. He called himself stupid, painfully taking slights and unkind words to heart.

Marie-Joseph also could become violently envious of those for whom study was simple. There were several times when his frustration boiled over and he felt like quitting.

His studies were not Joseph's only problem. Frankly, he was no one's idea of the ideal monk. To say that he couldn't carry a tune in a bucket is putting it mildly, and since the monks chanted the Divine Office several times a day, this was something of a problem. (Pity the poor ears of his fellow monks!) So was the fact that he had a tough time paying attention. "When I don't have a book, if I keep my eyes open, I become distracted; if I close them, I fall asleep."[4]

Additionally Joseph battled frequent thoughts against purity, and because of this and other perceived sins, he suffered from severe bouts of scrupulosity. To make matters worse, he was clumsy and had not one friend other than Fr. André.

Through Fr. André's gentle love and guidance, however, Joseph persevered. Father told him, "Look at the cross," and so Br. Marie-Joseph would spend hours meditating on the crucifix, on how Jesus, too, felt the depths of sadness, and how all but Mary and a handful of others abandoned him. This taught him to rely more on Jesus than himself, and this is what gradually led him to take as his motto, "All for Jesus through Mary."

Slowly Joseph began to not only get his lessons but also conquer his faults and grow in holiness. As a result he wrote some exceedingly beautiful things. For instance:

- "When a bad thought crosses my mind, if it remains in spite of me, I am not responsible for it.... For it to be a sin that must be confessed, I must have voluntarily lingered there."
- "I always remember that a short prayer from the bottom of one's heart, if one can do no better, is the most pleasing to God."
- "O Jesus, grant me the grace that I might be in continual conversation with You."
- "My God, I willingly turn over, with all my heart, to the souls in purgatory the merits of all the good works that I will do in the future, the indulgences I will earn, and the prayers in suffrage that will be offered for me after my death, and I place them all into the hands of the Immaculate Virgin Mary."[5]

How Br. Marie-Joseph persevered, how he kept trying, is inspiring. He faithfully and humbly did all that was asked of him. Sure, it was difficult, and, yes, he knew disappointment, even great disappointment. But people described him as happy, "always with a smile on his face."[6] Some say this is meekness.

His determination to become a priest finally came to fruition on October 12, 1902. Sadly, he had contracted tuberculosis by this time, although he had amazingly concealed it for several months, and it only became evident when he could no longer do so. When asked why he had kept his illness hidden, he remarkably replied that he didn't complain because he would look at the cross and think of how the Lord had suffered much more.[7]

"When I am no longer able to say Holy Mass," he told Fr. André, "the Heart of Jesus can draw me from this world, for I no longer have any attachment to the earth."[8]

Hoping to help him recover, his superiors sent Marie-Joseph back to the devoted care of his parents. After two months, however, it became clear that his end was near, and so he returned to his beloved monastery.

From this point his deterioration was both rapid and painful, and he could never get comfortable, in part because of the bedsores he developed. Compounding his agony, the infirmarian was his former theology professor. We do not know whether the man treated Fr. Cassant any better as he was dying than when he had been his student.

Fr. Cassant died on June 7, 1903. As of 2009, over twenty-two hundred people from around the world had attributed graces received to his intercession.

PRAYER

Holy Spirit, things often seem too tough, and we yearn for easier days. Sometimes we weep under the burdens we bear in this "valley of tears." Help us to profit by Bl. Marie-Joseph's example, to embrace the cross and not count the cost, to continue as Jesus did on the road to Calvary, one step at a time under its agonizing weight until we reach our appointed end. Through his prayers, give us confidence that you have a plan of good for us and not for evil, and help us to thereby trust in you always.

Saint Agostina Livia Pietrantoni

March 27, 1864–November 13, 1894

Beatified November 12, 1972

Canonized April 18, 1999

21

Olivia (also known as Livia) Pietrantoni is another martyr for chastity. Beyond that she shows the interconnection of the two greatest commandments, to love God with all your heart and to love your neighbor as yourself (see Matthew 22:35–40).

Born the second of eleven children to pious but poor parents in a little mountain village, Livia was almost always working. Because her parents were farmers and all the children were expected to help support the family, there was hardly any time for playing, and Livia attended school only sporadically. At age seven she helped transport sacks of sand and stone for construction of a nearby road. At twelve she harvested olives as a migrant farm worker.

That sort of work isn't enjoyable for adults, much less children, but Livia made the best of the situation. She became a kind of leader of the other children, teaching them catechism and looking after their spiritual and moral development. When overseers were harsh or picked on particular children, she stood up to them.

Because Livia was very pretty, her mother dreamed of getting her into a good marriage that would improve her lot in life. But from an early age—we don't know exactly when—Livia had a strong desire for God and discerned her religious vocation. Ironically, some accused her of trying to escape a life of hard work, to which she replied, "I wish to choose a congregation in which there is work both day and night."[1] After all, she later said, "we will lie down for such a long time after death that it is worthwhile to keep standing while we are alive. Let us work now; one day we will rest."[2]

The Sisters of Charity of St. Jeanne-Antide Thouret accepted Livia. On leaving her loving family, one biographer says, she "kissed the door of her house, traced the sign of the cross on it and left hurriedly."[3] She was twenty-two years old.

As a novice Livia took the name Agostina. Her postulancy was in Rome, at the beautiful, Byzantine-influenced Santa Maria in Cosmedin. Her superiors quickly realized how well she worked with the poor, and so they sent her to work at Santo Spirito Hospital.

In her new position Sr. Agostina was charitable "to the point of heroism,"[4] although this wasn't easy for her. The difficulty wasn't due to the work, which she was used to, but to the attitude many showed her. She had arrived at a time when Italy was becoming unified. This created a political situation that tended to set those who were faithful Christians against those who weren't.

As such, many of the patients and administrators were hostile to religion and anyone associated with it. The Capuchin Fathers had already been forced to leave the hospital, crucifixes had been taken from all the rooms, and there were no statues in the halls. The hospital was simply a bare, secular square. The administrators would have sent the sisters away too, but they feared public opinion. They could stay, they were told, but they were not to speak of God.

In this atmosphere of religious oppression, Sr. Agostina worked herself to the bone for eight years serving her patients, even living in the tubercular ward at a time when tuberculosis was an incurable and highly contagious disease. (She later caught TB, but prayers to Our Lady obtained a miraculous cure.) Forbidden to mention the holy name, she did the next best thing, which was to follow the dictum attributed to St. Francis: "Preach the gospel always; when necessary, use words." She showed Christ's love to each person, working tirelessly in a ward of six rooms with two hundred men in each.

Thus isolated in a small space, the men grew increasingly exasperated, a condition born of inactivity, which is never good for anyone. Many of them developed sullen natures; others fell into vulgarity. The stress of working with these venomous men was painful for the sisters and induced nausea in some. Sr. Agostina, however, tried to keep the proper attitude.

"I am here by the special grace of God," she wrote. "These men are not bad, just sick. How much comfort there is in the thought that, in them, I serve Jesus Christ."[5] Finding a secret spot in the hospital, she would use her free time to pray and offer up these souls to Our Lady, constantly interceding for their conversion to her divine Son.

Perhaps because of her diligence in service, Sr. Agostina apparently didn't see the serious threat that awaited her in Joseph Romanelli, who made abuse into an art form. His invectives, garden variety at first, steadily became worse. He swore, was hostile and stiff-necked, and had no compunction about grabbing and groping the women working in the hospital. To Sr. Agostina's credit, the worse he was to her, the better she was to him. She was especially nice to his blind mother when she came to visit.

Finally the hospital administration had had enough of Romanelli's rudeness. Sick or not, he was forced to leave.

Enraged and insane, Romanelli looked for someone to blame, and he chose Sr. Agostina, the one person who had never been anything but loving toward him. He sent her notes saying, "I will kill you with my own hands," and, "You only have a month to live!"[6]

On November 13, 1894, Romanelli sneaked back into the hospital and called Sr. Agostina toward the kitchen. When she came into a corridor from which there was no escape, he tried to rape her, and when she resisted, he stabbed her repeatedly.

As she lay dying a martyr of love, her superior asked her, "Do you forgive him?"[7] Her weak smile, mustered with the last slivers of life left in her, answered Mother's question.

God does bring good out of evil. Sr. Agostina's murder was a moment of grace for the people of Rome. It is said the event helped embolden them against the antireligious sentiment of the age and reawakened in many the power of prayer and the gospel to change lives. Martyrdom speaks a language in even the hardest of hearts.

During Sr. Agostina's funeral procession, an adolescent girl asked her mother the meaning of the word *martyr*. Her mother replied, "A martyr is one who writes the things of God with his blood."[8]

PRAYER

Dear God, all of us face people in our lives who are difficult or whom we don't like. Help us to imitate St. Agostina's heroic charity in order to bring your love to a fallen world.

Blessed Emperor Karl I

August 17, 1887–April 1, 1922
Beatified October 3, 2004

When people are in dire need—when they have lost their jobs, their homes, everything they thought was safe and secure—they are often tempted to blame God and despair. While Emperor Karl I Habsburg knew this sense of loss, his actions in the situation make him a comforting and inspiring example for this age.

Karl's royalty did not guarantee a fairy-tale home life. Although affectionate with her young boy, his devout mother was deeply affected by the constant philandering of her husband, who was known as Oscar the Gorgeous. Additionally this man never did anything other than the minimum required of a husband and father. As a result the couple's marriage was entirely loveless and thus difficult, which occasionally made their home the same.

Furthermore, since he was in line for the throne, Karl was not permitted to do anything remotely dangerous. And while his mother took him to daily Mass, took responsibility for his catechesis, and spent time with him each day, Karl was mostly raised by governesses and tutors, including Count Georg Wallis, who, while he loved Karl, was overly strict with him.

Karl developed a deep faith life at an early age, and for most of his youth, he was consumed by the desire to become a saint.

Every time he passed a church, he stopped in to pray, a habit he never lost. When a local house burned down, he emptied his piggy bank for the bereft family.

On entering the military, however, Karl was on his own for the first time, and his pursuit of holy perfection slackened due to some bad advice from his uncle Archduke Franz Ferdinand. As a result, he carelessly discarded his virginity, and while his failures of chastity only happened a few times, he later said recalling these episodes "always filled him with remorse and disgust."[1]

The woman he eventually married was a gorgeous Italian named Princess Zita of Bourbon-Parma, whose own family seemed to be perfect. Not only were they devout, but they were actually happy with one another. Karl saw in Zita a woman with whom home life could be serene and who could help him become a saint. Shortly after saying, "I do," he turned to her and said, "Now we must help each other get to heaven."[2]

With Franz Ferdinand's assassination in Sarajevo, Karl became the heir apparent. His uncle's assassination also started World War I, and from the conflict's start until Karl's ascension to the throne, he served as a military commander and won some important victories. But having seen war firsthand, he absolutely hated it, and when he became emperor after his great-uncle Emperor Franz Joseph I's death, he diligently tried to make peace. Had people listened to him, millions of lives would have been saved. As it was his efforts were mischaracterized and used to ridicule him, this good man who was the only ruler to ban the use of poison gas.

The emperor also tried to implement principles of Catholic social teaching during his reign. What laws he was able to pass made life easier for the working class, and he provided the best example himself by raising the salaries of the government's day laborers.

No good deed goes unpunished, however, and Karl's reward for his ceaseless attempts to do right was to suffer the worst lies: that he was unfaithful, that he used prostitutes, that he was a drunk. These accusations hurt him, but they had the benefit of strengthening his spiritual life. Even before this he was confessing each week and praying the psalms daily. He had consecrated his children to the Virgin Mary and his household to Jesus' Sacred Heart, and he had taught his children their prayers. He was a good, virtuous man, the sort of leader for which our age desperately thirsts.

As the war lingered and terrible hardship set in, Karl did all he could to make his people's plight less difficult, organizing soup kitchens, using his own horses to haul coal, and giving away his own wealth to what some believe was an imprudent extent. He even made the royal household live on war rations. Some high-ranking officers later said that the food on the front lines was better than that at the imperial table.

For some time prior to the war, Karl's Austro-Hungarian Empire had been beset by factions and independence movements. With the war's end, and with the United States supporting these independence movements, the empire disintegrated. Even his own Austria declared itself an independent republic, and so he effectively abdicated, although he never used that term. In his mind this was merely a temporary withdrawal from governing until such time as the future government and his role in it could be decided.

At first Karl went to Switzerland. He hoped to regain power from exile, but Austria passed a law banning the Habsburgs from even entering the country unless they renounced their royal prerogatives. Since Karl wholeheartedly believed that, like the papacy, his office was truly God-given and that he had no right to resign, he refused.

Karl did have two chances to regain the throne in Hungary. The first ended when his power-hungry regent, Admiral Horthy, convinced him the timing was not right. He stopped the second chance when he saw that the threat of civil war was unavoidable, pitting the loyalist army against poorly armed university students. Horthy had lied to the students, telling them Slovak soldiers disguised as Hungarian soldiers had taken Karl and Zita prisoner. Karl withdrew because, according to his vice postulator, he believed "the return of his crown was not worth the spilling of a single drop of Hungarian blood."[3]

When the Hungarian Cardinal János Csernoch went to Karl on behalf of the British to persuade him to renounce his crown outright, Karl, whose hair had turned gray by this time, replied, "As crowned king, I not only have a right, I also have a duty.... With the last breath of my life I must take the path of duty."[4]

One last chance was held out to him to regain royal power: He would have to liberalize morality laws, such as those concerning marriage. But remembering our Lord's words, "What profits a man if he gains the world but loses his soul?" he said no.

In 1922 the Allies exiled Karl and his family to the Portuguese island of Madeira, where he spent the last five months of his life in poverty. Although he had planned to sell his family's jewels and live on the proceeds, these had been stolen by a banker entrusted with their care while the Habsburgs were in Switzerland.

A wealthy man gave the family the use of a summer house in the mountains, but it was not really fit for winter habitation.

Water dripped down the walls because of the humidity, and the chimney smoked. While they had some domestic help, this family that had never had to cook, clean, or perform other mundane chores now had to completely provide for themselves

On the last New Year's Eve of his life, while he, his wife, and another couple were praying the *Te Deum*, all but Karl started sobbing. Because his relationship with God and his resolution to live *Fiat voluntas tua* ("Thy will be done") had become so complete, he alone finished this moving prayer of thanks.

Walking home from town one foggy morning, Karl caught a cold that grew into pneumonia. It quickly became evident that, with no antibiotics and living in a drafty house, the illness would prove fatal. Looking at the crucifix held by Zita, his last words were "Thy will be done.... Yes.... Yes.... As you will it.... Jesus!"[5] His epitaph reads, *Fiat voluntas tua.*

In a fitting testimony to the love he and his wife shared, their hearts are buried together at a monastery in Switzerland. Four of his eight children were still alive at the time of his beatification, and they were present at the ceremony. There Pope John Paul II stated that in Karl God had given the world a man whose "chief concern was to follow the Christian vocation to holiness."[6]

PRAYER

Dear Lord, our world needs more leaders like Bl. Karl. Through his prayers help all men to be strong and courageous leaders who sincerely desire Fiat voluntas tua. *And help those who have fallen on hard times take comfort and courage from his example.*

Blessed Edward Poppe

December 18, 1890–June 10, 1924

Beatified October 3, 1999

23

Many know about the 1996 *New York Times* poll that revealed that 70 percent of self-identified Catholics believe the Eucharist is merely a "symbolic reminder" of Jesus. A more recent survey places that number at only 43 percent.[1] Regardless of the precise figure, this high level of disbelief is a travesty, for the Church teaches the Eucharist is not just a symbol but really the Body, Blood, Soul, and Divinity of Jesus Christ. Indeed, she goes so far as to call it "the source and summit" of Christian life.[2]

Given the disparity between the two understandings, it would seem we have something of a problem. One way to correct this might be to study the example of Edward Poppe, who helped the youngest members of the Church develop a special love for our Lord in the Blessed Sacrament.

Edward was raised in a Flemish Catholic family, and both his parents were good, solid examples of how people should live their faith. For instance, while his father often struggled to keep his bakery afloat, Mr. Poppe's response to this or any other difficulty was almost like a mantra: "We must always be satisfied with the will of God."[3] For her part his mother attended daily Mass.

She needed the graces that came from this because Edward was a difficult child. He was hyperactive, easily broke things, pestered his sisters, got into mischief, and could be disobedient. He also had a tendency to eat his dad's profits (he had a *big* sweet tooth). Still, what most people noticed was his happy nature and precocious honesty.

Edward's behavior experienced a marked change after his first confession, First Communion, and confirmation, all at age twelve. He settled down and matured, and two years later his father brought him into the business. He wanted his son to follow in his footsteps, which Edward outwardly seemed ready to do. Unbeknown to his father, however, he had already set his heart on becoming a priest. When this became evident his dad said, "I prefer what God wants. Besides, let's not be selfish. God has not given us our children for ourselves."[4]

And so Edward entered the minor seminary at age fourteen. A year later Mr. Poppe passed away, and Edward resigned himself to going back home and supporting his family. That was when he learned his father's dying wish: that he stay in school. We'll be fine, his mother told him.

Edward's studies were interrupted, however, when he was called to military service. On discovering he was a seminarian, his fellow soldiers mocked him. They also taunted him by engaging in a level of immorality that can only be compared to a demonic assault. They used foul language, described "conquests" in his hearing, and generally let no opportunity to abuse his moral sensibilities go by. He described this time as "a hell."[5] In addition he was unable to fulfill his Sunday obligation to attend Mass each week, which for him was the worst suffering of all.

But here is how God works in mysterious ways: Without this experience Edward never would have gained an invaluable window into the human condition. He came to understand that these comrades, while coarse on the outside, were really searching for God, although they might have laughed if he had told them that. Once he comprehended this, he was able to befriend them and even offer spiritual counsel. Thus years later, when he took over the training of seminarians and religious fulfilling their military obligation, he knew how to guide them—and by extension their fellow soldiers—in a way he otherwise could not have.

After Edward's demobilization he reengaged in his studies with great vigor. But when a priest told him, "Your enthusiasm is common among young seminarians.... After ten years of priesthood, the reality of life completely extinguishes this illusion,"[6] it caused him to doubt his vocation. He couldn't pray, he started finding faults in every facet of his life, and he doubted God's love for him.

To help him combat this growing despair, his spiritual director told him, "Say often, 'Lord, I believe, but help me.'"[7] He also counseled him to focus on the crucifix and the sufferings it exemplifies. Doing this, Edward eventually regained his former fervor, which was also helped by his joining *Filioli Caritatis*, a group of young priests and seminarians aiming for priestly sanctity

His studies were interrupted again by World War I, in which he served as a nurse. He cared for so many wounded and dying soldiers that he collapsed from exhaustion. The priest who nursed him back to health had a deep devotion to St. Joseph and encouraged Edward to ask the Guardian of the Redeemer for a quick recovery, which he received.

Finally ordained in 1916, Edward's first appointment was to a new parish where most people didn't practice their faith. He decided that if the people would not come to him, he would meet them in the streets. He gave holy cards to children and greeted workers as they left their factories.

At first people ignored him, but then they started inviting him into their homes. There he saw heart-wrenching poverty. He gave whatever he could, and this generosity helped melt away the anti-clericalism that seems endemic to Europeans in Catholic countries. It also gave him the opportunity to preach Christ, which was his joy.

Edward's pastor, however, thought he was wasting his time on the rabble. Better, he said, to concentrate on saving the faithful rather than going after the lost sheep. "Humanly speaking, it's discouraging for the heart of a priest" to hear such things, the young priest wrote.[8]

One thing that helped him regain heart is what we now call youth ministry. By convincing some children that those who rose early were "the bravest," he was able to get two hundred of them to attend 7:00 AM Mass and Benediction during summer vacation. He little by little conceived of the League of Communion, which would bring together children who love Jesus in order to form them into his true disciples. The founding principle was that even children can handle the full gospel and can reach the Christian perfection proper to their state in life through the help of graces from the Eucharist.

As a result many children received their First Communion who otherwise would not have. This helped the "rabble" start practicing their faith again: The adults were led to piety by their children.

As Edward himself wrote, none of this would have been possible without prayer. "According to the divine plan, action must be fed with prayer. The interior life is the wellspring of the apostolate…. Do not believe in the slogan, 'The priest is sanctified in sanctifying others'—it's an illusion. The real formula is, 'Sanctify yourself in order to sanctify others.'"[9]

Yet even with prayer all of these apostolic activities exhausted Father, and he was told to lie in bed for thirty days. When he had recovered, he wanted to pick up where he had left off, but his pastor, fearing a relapse, told him to break off the Communion League meetings, the youth groups, and teaching CCD. A reluctant Fr. Poppe submitted. He wrote:

> Suffer and obey. Is the servant greater than his Master? We are intelligent, we understand how to conceive and organize our works, we have foresight and initiative; and we even burn with zeal. But Jesus was more intelligent and more zealous, had more foresight, and understood more than do we! His zeal was a consuming fire. He knew how to order His life much better than we do.... And yet Jesus obeyed Joseph and Mary in everything. He left the last word to authority—over the course of thirty years, He recognized and taught the value of authority. The price of obedience rises beyond all estimation when we think that Jesus, who submitted Himself, was God. His entire life, as a child and as a young man, His mission and His death—a death on the Cross—was a great act of obedience.[10]

It seems his pastor's concerns were well-founded, for even without his apostolic works, Fr. Poppe's health failed again. His bishop named him director of a community of women religious in a nearby village, thinking this service would be less stressful than pastoral work. Fr. Poppe and the village priest began an hour of adoration each week, and slowly villagers joined them, beginning again with the children.

Father then suffered two heart attacks, and though he recovered, illness greatly slowed him down. Six months later he experienced yet another heart attack, and another the next month. He sensed this was God's way of telling him he was not long for the world.

Confined to his bed and hating the boredom and inactivity, he took up a writing apostolate in which he counseled against the Marxism, secularism, and materialism that threatened to disrupt the Church and consume society. Having passed the winter in this way, he succumbed to a stroke in the early summer of 1924. He was thirty-three.

The epitaph of this man whose ideal was holiness and who hated mediocrity reads, "Better to die than to serve God by halves."[11]

PRAYER

Sweet Jesus, you not only humbled yourself by being born in an impoverished stable, but you continue to humble yourself by remaining with us under the appearance of bread, which invites condescension, abuse, and even disbelief among your followers. Help us to see you anew in the Eucharist and, through the prayers of Blessed Edward Poppe, to serve you with ever-greater zeal.

Blessed Anna Schäffer

February 18, 1882–October 5, 1925
Beatified March 7, 1999

24

Most people who experience martyrdom—literally, witnessing to their faith by giving their lives—do so in an instant. The ax falls, the rifle cracks, and the witness is accomplished. Others, such as Anna Schäffer, suffer their martyrdom over a much longer period of time.

Born into a deeply religious family, Anna was a good student and a remarkably quiet, very devout girl. Indeed, by the time of her First Communion at age eleven, she wanted to save souls for her beloved Jesus as a missionary. However, when her dad died in 1896, and with her family not being well off to begin with, she had to go to work as a maid to earn the dowry necessary for entrance into the convent.

On February 4, 1901, while she was working at a logging house, the stovepipe from the laundry boiler came undone. Trying to fix it, Anna slipped and fell up to her knees into a roiling cauldron of lye. Instead of trying to pull her out, her coworker panicked and ran to find help, which took several minutes. Anna was finally put in a cart and taken to a hospital over four miles away. It took another several hours for the doctor to begin surgery, and the surgery itself, at a time before anesthesia was common, took another two hours.

The doctors were able to cauterize Anna's wounds, and they eventually performed over thirty skin grafts on her legs. But her legs never healed. In fact they became essentially useless, and she was bedridden the rest of her life. Because she could no longer work, she was even more severely impoverished than before.

At first, like any normal person, she hated her situation. For many years, possibly eight or nine—the exact length of time is uncertain—she bitterly complained and ceaselessly prayed for a miraculous cure. Every moment of that time was spent in the same bed feeling trapped and sorry for herself, fighting her situation, railing against it, incessantly begging God for a miracle and occasionally growing angry with him for not waving his hand and giving it. It must have been hell.

Through it all, Anna's kind and patient parish priest and spiritual director, Fr. Rieger, brought her the Eucharist on an almost daily basis. Through his persistent encouragement and the grace of the sacrament, she learned in this difficult school of suffering to recognize and accept God's will and to do so with joy. She realized that, although she had wanted to serve Christ as a missionary sister, she could do just as much for souls by joining her sufferings to his (see Colossians 1:24). Again, this took a long time to happen, nearly a decade.

This change was solidified in the fall of 1910, when Anna began having extraordinary visions of St. Francis, Our Lady, and Christ. These convinced her to join her life to the cross and offer it in reparation for the sins of the world. On October 4, 1910, Christ showed he accepted her offer by giving her the stigmata on her feet, hands, and head. These were not very discernible, and she took care to hide what evidence there was of them.

Anna launched an apostolate that focused on intercessory prayer, words of comfort, and letter writing. Over the rest of her life, she filled twelve notebooks with her spiritual thoughts and wrote over 180 letters. The postulator for her cause, Domvikar Georg Schwager, wrote, "Anna drew her strength [for this mission] from the Holy Eucharist. Therein she found her comfort, her joy, and also the courage to offer up her suffering for the conversion of sinners and for the Church."[1]

On April 25, 1923, while experiencing a vision of the first Good Friday, Anna's condition took a turn for the worse. Her legs became completely paralyzed, and she experienced terrible cramping from a spinal condition. Later she developed rectal cancer. A fall from her bed some weeks later resulted in a brain injury that left her impaired in both sight and speech.

Anna lived the rest of her days in unbelievable physical pain. People marveled at how she could endure. Her last actions were to make the Sign of the Cross and pray, "Jesus, I love you."

According to her postulator,

> The essential thing in the life of Anna Schäffer is her great readiness to abandon herself completely to the will of God, which was enabled and strengthened by the Eucharist. Often she would say, "My God, I thank you; my God, I love you." We should gladly repeat this prayer of hers, in order to thus gratefully deepen our own love for God despite the cross and suffering that come to us.[2]

PRAYER

Lord Jesus, so often we are told suffering is worthless. But what if you had not given Bl. Anna Schäffer this cross for twenty-five years? How many souls were saved by her joining her sufferings to your cross for their salvation? Your will is mysterious, but by our accepting it, by being patient and waiting on you to reveal your purposes, you will work miracles with our lives that we cannot even imagine. Help us to understand and remember this in times of trial and to do so with joy.

Blessed Pina Suriano

February 18, 1915–May 19, 1950
Beatified September 5, 2004

25

There are times when we wonder, "What is God's plan for me?"
Goals we set and desires we have, which seem to make total sense
from a spiritual or religious perspective, come to absolutely nothing. In the end we ask, "Why, Lord? I was doing this for *you*."

To have this reaction is only natural, but the question is, how
do we move forward? Do we pout in misery or, like Pina Suriano,
love God all the more?

Pina was born in Sicily and given the name Giuseppina. Her
religious parents raised her to always perceive God's presence. At
age twelve she started taking part in parish activities and in
Catholic Action, an organization of laity extant in some parts of
Europe that tries to exert a Catholic influence on society. These
activities helped stoke her already deep love for the faith, the
result of which was that she completely threw herself into the
spiritual life.

This flowering of her ardor for God implanted in Pina a desire
to enter a convent. She and some friends even conceived a plan
to found a religious order of their own. Surprisingly, however,
Pina's mother opposed her entering religious life. In fact she
opposed all her religious activities, because she thought it made

Pina a less attractive candidate for marriage. The irony is that Pina's religious activities enabled her inner beauty to shine, making this gorgeous young woman even more attractive. She never lacked for marriage offers.

Pina repeatedly made it known that she only wanted Christ for her spouse, but her family would not budge. "Better to have a dead daughter than one who was a nun," they told her.[1] So while she recognized her vocation—and her spiritual director confirmed it—she could not give herself to it, and Pina often felt depressed as a result.

In her diary she poured out her heart:

> Who can know of this drawn out and painful martyrdom I live and the tears I shed in silence? My soul cries out and is in danger of falling into a bottomless pit.... It is a constant martyrdom of the heart.... I feel alone and without help, human or divine, abandoned even by the One who is my entire life.... I offer all this up to him.[2]

Starting in 1932, Pina made a vow of chastity that she renewed each month, and to her parents' consternation, she continued to decline marriage offers. Finally, in 1940, her parents relented and gave her permission to become a religious, and she entered the Daughters of St. Anne with great joy. Just eight days later, however, doctors diagnosed her with a serious heart problem. She had to leave the convent.

Instead of being morose about this tragic turn of events, Pina wrote, "Jesus, make me more and more your own. Jesus, I want to live and die with you and for you."[3]

Eight years later, with the permission of her spiritual director, Pina and four friends told God they would accept any sufferings he might choose to send them for the sanctification of priests. Not long after this she began suffering from rheumatic arthritis. She wrote,

> The first offer that I make to the Lord will be bitter pain, the great torture of my soul [for her unrealized vocation]. I will be happy, if this is the will of the Lord, that the religious life remain for me a dream.... I will thank the Lord and remain happy even in the midst of this martyrdom.... I will be ready to suffer all physical, moral and spiritual torment.[4]

On Friday, May 19, 1950, as she prepared to go to Mass, Pina suffered a fatal heart attack. She was thirty-five years old.

PRAYER

Lord, how inscrutable are your ways. Bl. Pina wanted only you, yet on the face of it, you rejected her holy offer. You wanted something else from her. Thank you for giving her the grace to show us what to do when things don't work out the way we want. We praise you for her beautiful example of total acceptance and love for your holy will. Through her prayers, may we too accept that will, come what may.

Blessed Bartolo Longo
February 10, 1841–October 5, 1926
Beatified October 26, 1980

26

Many look at the terrible things they have done in their lives and despair that God could *ever* forgive them. But he forgave a former Satanic priest named Bartolo Longo; surely he can forgive anybody.

Bartolo came from a devout and wealthy family who prayed the rosary daily and never missed Mass. When he was ten years old, however, the death of his mother caused him to doubt God's goodness, and he started drifting away from the faith. Then in high school, wanting to know which course current events would take, he and some classmates consulted a soothsayer. This was the first of his many experiences with the occult.

By the time Bartolo entered the University of Naples, he was ripe for conversion to Satanism. The school purposefully taught courses that undermined the Christian faith, including one course taught by a fallen-away priest that questioned whether Christ was God.

Such experiences utterly demolished Bartolo's faith. As a result, he started frequenting fortune-tellers, which made him thirst for occult knowledge. He adopted a Satanic belief system, and after some study he was ordained a Satanic priest.

As time went on, however, Longo found himself increasingly plagued by a variety of mental and physical maladies, including depression and diabolical visions. His appearance, some sources say, was itself demonic: He looked haggard, and his eyes were like black coals. His life was guided by his "spirit angel's" directions, which made him venomously anti-Catholic and blasphemous.

Recognizing that something was not right, Bartolo sought out his good friend Professor Vincenzo Pepe. This man had not seen Bartolo since before his ordination and now did not recognize him. He helped him see that Satanism wasn't incidental to his problem but the very cause of it. Pepe sent him to Fr. Alberto Radente, who became his lifelong spiritual director.

Over the next month, in a protracted confession, Bartolo detailed his sins as a Satanic priest. On the Feast of the Sacred Heart in 1865, after receiving absolution from Fr. Radente, he received Holy Communion.

From then on Bartolo Longo dedicated himself to spiritual and corporal works of mercy, assisting Bl. Caterina Volpicelli and the priest Bl. Ludovico da Casoria, who today is called the "Mother Teresa of Naples" because of his work with the poor. Many understandably regarded Bartolo poorly because he had been a Satanic priest. We can imagine his feeling like St. Paul after his conversion, distrusted and an outcast. But he found strength in the rosary, and he received an internal grace to know that those who promoted this Christ-centered prayer would receive spiritual blessings.

While doing legal business in Pompeii, Bartolo was shocked by conditions there. He commonly saw people and livestock living in the same hovel. The spiritual impoverishment was worse: Only 5 percent of the two thousand villagers ever went to the run-down, vermin-infested church and that was when the priest actually offered the sacraments. They knew nothing of their faith, believed in a mixture of skewed ideas and superstitions, and even had recourse to witches and mediums. Having just left the darkness of Satan, it astounded and saddened Bartolo that these people would neglect and abuse the Church's great gifts.

Recalling the promise that if one promoted the rosary, one would receive blessings, he made it his life's work to improve this woeful situation. First he restored the dilapidated church. Then he organized a celebration, replete with fireworks, races, and music, to honor Our Lady of the Rosary on her feast.

Bartolo found in the church an old painting of Our Lady of the Rosary: The canvas was moth-eaten and the paint chipped in many places, and the figures were inartfully drawn. Indeed, he later wrote that the figure of St. Dominic looked like "an idiot." He paid for the painting's restoration, which was very well done. If you go to Pompeii today, this is the painting you will see.

He taught people their catechism and how to pray the rosary. Miracles began happening. The villagers thronged to the church, and people from around the nation donated millions of lire for Bartolo's efforts to expand the church. He published a magazine devoted to spreading good works, and it became the largest, most well-read journal in the country.

"We wanted only to provide for the religious life of poor peasants," he later wrote. "We succeeded instead in producing a truly universal movement of faith, a Catholic movement, Catholic [that is, universal] just as the Church is."[1]

As the small village church could not hold all the pilgrims, Bartolo began to build a larger one, which was consecrated in 1876. Surrounding it he built schools for poor children, nurseries for impoverished families, orphanages, and places where young people could learn a trade.

Bartolo had a close working relationship with his longtime benefactress, Countess Marianna de Fusco. People gossiped about the nature of the relationship, and so their friend Pope Leo XIII counseled them to marry. They remained celibate, however, and both continued providing charity to orphans, the poor, and prisoners.

Bartolo promoted the rosary until his death. Indeed, he was praying this prayer when he died from exhaustion at age eighty-five.

PRAYER

God our Father, we have all done wrong in our lives, but your mercy knows no bounds. Forgive us our countless sins, dear Lord, and through Bl. Bartolo's prayers, may we be ever-shining lights that bear witness to your love, goodness, and unfathomable mercy.

Blessed Miguel Pro
    January 13, 1891–November 23, 1927
    Beatified September 25, 1988

27

Just before he ascended into heaven, Jesus told his followers, "Go therefore and make disciples of all nations" (Matthew 28:19). But evangelization is rarely an easy thing, and many of us act as though we are afraid of getting arrested if we do it. For Fr. Miguel Pro arrest was a very real possibility, and yet he was fearless in spreading the gospel.

Miguel was the third of eleven children born to a Mexican business executive and his wife. The family was a happy one and devout in its practice of the faith, which was not easy for Mexicans at the time.

This may seem odd because most of us conceive of Mexico as a devout land filled with pious people, and that is to a great extent true. But since around 1850 the country has sometimes been ruled by people who passionately hate the Church, so much so that campaigns have broken out against her and her faithful on a number of occasions. One response to this was the Cristero War (1926–1929), an insurrection by faithful Catholics against the Masonic government's oppression. The government's reaction was brutal, and this gives us the context for our story.

As Miguel grew from a very funny, although sometimes very bratty, child into a young man, he did the normal things most young men do; he even had a girlfriend. Eventually, however, he discerned a priestly vocation, and so he entered the Jesuits in 1911. The aforementioned persecutions forced him and hundreds of others to flee in 1914. He pursued his schooling in California, Spain, Nicaragua, and finally Belgium, where he was ordained on August 31, 1925. Then he returned to his native land.

In the meantime the Masons had passed the 1917 Constitution, which made it illegal for priests to administer the sacraments or do any pastoral work, such as retreats, sick calls, and processions. A 1926 law fined priests five hundred pesos ($2,900 in today's American dollars) for wearing clerical garb in public. Some local governors cleared priests entirely out of their states.

Thus from the beginning of his priesthood, Miguel had to practice his vocation in secret. A master of disguises, he would dress as a street cleaner or a beggar in order to visit homes and administer the sacraments. Once he dressed as a police officer to enter a jail and administer last rites to some condemned men. He would dress as a driver and hold retreats for mechanics.

While saying Mass in a house once, a lookout warned everyone the police were on the way. Fr. Pro was wearing a police inspector's uniform under his vestments, so he slipped out the rear, doubled back to the house, and castigated the man in charge for not finding that "rascal Pro."

Another time, using a taxi as a getaway car and with the police in hot pursuit, Miguel told the driver to slow down as he turned the corner. Father rolled out of the car and, seeing a pretty girl headed in the opposite direction, told her, "Give me your arm!"

He explained, "I am a priest," and the startled girl understood the situation. The two walked arm-in-arm toward his pursuers, who passed them by. After all, why would a priest be walking with a girl?

Fr. Miguel would not let unjust laws deter his God-given vocation to make disciples. This helps explain his tireless and fearless efforts and also the exuberant joy that this clown of God exhibited in giving his all for he who is all.

An acquaintance had used Miguel's brother's car in an assassination attempt on the president. While knowing the priest was not involved, the police nonetheless used this as a pretext to arrest him. At a kangaroo court they sentenced him to death.

On the morning of his execution, Fr. Miguel bravely walked to the place where he was to stand. He blessed his executioners, took a moment to pray, stretched out his arms as did Christ on the cross, and shouted his last words, *Viva Cristo Rey!* ("Long live Christ the King!"). Thus he received the bullets that rendered him a martyr.

PRAYER

Father in heaven, we for whom practicing and preaching our faith is perfectly legal sometimes act as if it was not in that we fear to share it. Help us to follow Fr. Miguel Pro's fearless example by giving all to spread your kingdom.

Blessed José Luis Sánchez del Río

March 28, 1913–February 10, 1928

Beatified November 20, 2005

28

When we think of martyrs, we typically think of priests, religious, and lay adults. However, it is possible even for a child to give his life for Christ, as we see in the case of José Luis Sánchez del Río.

Hailing from a small town in Mexico, José was just another young boy doing young boy things and dreaming young boy dreams. He was fascinated by horses, played marbles, and loved to hunt doves with his friends. While poor in material possessions, his family was rich in their faith, and his parents showed him that the important things in life are faith, hope, and love toward all, friend and stranger.

That idyllic boyhood ended when José was twelve and the Cristero War commenced. This was a war fought by faithful Catholic Mexicans against the Masonic and anticlerical policies of their government, which had led to the abolition of religious orders; the closing of seminaries, monasteries, convents, and churches; the confiscation of church property; and the harassment and even murder of faithful Catholics. It is said that the people would wake in the morning, go out to their fields, and find the corpses of those whom the *federales* had executed during the night.

Seeing his brothers join the cause to liberate their holy religion, the thirteen-year-old José wanted to enlist as well, but his parents discouraged him, and General Prudencio Mendoza rejected him because of his youth. But like a modern-day David, the boy insisted, and his parents and Mendoza finally relented.

On February 5, 1928, in a battle in which federal forces outnumbered the Cristeros ten to one, government soldiers captured José and held him prisoner in the baptistery of the local church. While he was imprisoned, he saw that Rafael Picasso, the captain, had a bunch of roosters running around in the church. He said to himself, "Look at this mess. This idiot has turned the church into a chicken coop!" He took the roosters by the necks and killed them. He hung their bodies from the Communion rail.

The commander was incensed on discovering this and threatened to end the boy's life right there. José bravely responded, "The house of God is for praying, not for sheltering animals."[1]

Normally the federal forces would simply shoot captured Cristeros or hang them from a tree, but, possibly on account of his tender age, they gave José some time to reflect upon his fate. They hoped to scare him into renouncing his Catholic faith to save his life. To further frighten the boy, they made him prepare the noose for another Cristero, whom they then hanged in his presence. But like the martyrs of past centuries, José only urged the dying man to remember that to lose one's earthly life for Christ was to gain eternal life. "We will meet again in heaven," he told him.[2]

Meanwhile, José's father tried to raise the ransom of five thousand gold pesos (thirty thousand dollars in today's currency), but his poverty made this impossible. He offered everything he owned, but the general in charge refused.

Having had José for almost a week, and seeing no signs of his relenting, the government soldiers' patience was spent. Around 11:00 PM on February 10, they started the process of his execution by cutting off the bottoms of his feet and then marching him through the town's cobbled streets toward the cemetery. There his captors told him, "If you shout, 'Death to Christ the King,' we will spare your life." In response he loudly shouted, "*Viva Cristo Rey!* (Long live Christ the King!),"[3] even while his assassins stabbed him.

The soldiers stabbed José with bayonets because they didn't want the sound of gunshots waking the villagers, but his screams were doing just that, so the captain killed him with a bullet to the head. With his last bit of strength, José traced a cross in the ground, and he died kissing it.

PRAYER

Dear Lord, even a youth can comprehend that eternal life is far more valuable than this one, and that it would be better to die than to reject you, who saved us from our sins and bought our eternal life with so high a price. You may not call us to martyrdom, but through the example and prayers of Bl. José, let us be as faithful to you as any martyr has ever been.

Blessed Ivan Merz

December 16, 1896–May 10, 1928

Beatified June 22, 2003

29

Very few people are born saints. For most of us sanctity is a struggle, and too often it seems like we cannot win. We grow discouraged to the point where we think, "Why bother?"

Ivan Merz knew these struggles. He knew them deeply. He may have felt like giving up. Yet he persevered, and his example shows that holiness is possible for us all.

Ivan's parents were what we would today call "cafeteria Catholics." They followed Church teachings that were to their liking and loved material things. They evidently believed in the "eighth sacrament" of holy osmosis: The one in which you drop your child off at religious education classes and expect the faith to sink in without any effort on your part.

Luckily for Ivan, he had Dr. Ljubomir Marakovic for his teacher. This man inspired in him a deep love for Christ and his Church and even prompted him to begin his spiritual diary. This book reveals how Ivan fought to grow in holiness and conquer his sinfulness. It also shows how he struggled with the questions of love, pain, and death.

Wanting a good place for him in the world, Ivan's parents forced him to join the military academy in 1914. He left after three months, however, both because he wasn't cut out to be an officer and because of the moral corruption he found there. What Ivan saw of the empty and unhappy lives of those who thought themselves "free" by virtue of their rejection of Christianity's "rules" made the Christian life's true freedom even more attractive to him.

Ivan started his university studies but was soon drafted into the Austrian army. He spent the years 1916 to 1918 at the Italian front during World War I. His spiritual diary records that this was the time of his deepest spiritual doubt. "There is no Holy Eucharist," he wrote. "I am living as a pagan or as a beast, as if the *Agnus* [that is, the Lamb of God] was no more in the center of the universe, as if He did not exist at all."[1]

Through patient prayer, however, this spiritual doubt passed, and Ivan redoubled his spiritual efforts and even fasted at the front. He wrote that "there is no spiritual life without fasting."[2]

"Oh God," he wrote at the time, "burn all the parasites of sin that have crept into my soul with the flame of your mercy, so that I can appear before you good and holy; [inspire me to live with] a holy joy and an extraordinary will."[3]

When the war ended, Ivan went back to school, and after earning his philosophy doctorate from the University of Zagreb, he taught in that great city's archepiscopal high school. In his off hours he worked with youth and encouraged them to know and love the Mass and to more frequently access the sacraments.

Croatia was experiencing a remarkable period of religious activity and fervor in the 1920s, so in a sense Ivan's activities weren't unusual. What made him special was his unique capacity to show young people how to live for Christ in the performance of ordinary daily duties. He demonstrated that sanctity is the purview not just of consecrated religious and priests but of us all. Indeed, he taught his students that laypeople have opportunities to sanctify their lives and the world that priests and religious often don't.

Ivan's ability to serve came from the hours he spent in prayer each day: in adoration, with the breviary, and especially with the rosary. "When life is hard for you and when you meet with trouble," Ivan told his students, "take the rosary of Our Lady, and it will comfort you and give you strength to endure all in peace with a complete surrender to the will of God."[4] But the deepest source of Ivan's holiness was the Eucharist, which he received daily. Taking the advice of Pope St. Pius X, he didn't merely attend Mass but fervently prayed it.

This undoubtedly helped him with his pledge of lifelong celibacy. According to his postulator, Fr. Bozidar Nagy, Ivan was a regular man with regular attractions. At sixteen he even had a sweetheart with whom he was deeply in love, and her death left a "profound wound [in] his soul."[5] His diary speaks of this and "his struggle to preserve [his] chastity."[6]

"It is very interesting seeing his development in this sense," says Fr. Nagy. "In the last years of his life, he was completely liberated of sexual temptation because grace completely pervaded his soul."[7]

Some people thought Ivan was "too holy," and his efforts to help youth were first met with resistance. But good wins over evil, and holiness is ultimately the most attractive thing on earth. Eventually his efforts were not only accepted but embraced.

All his life Ivan had bad teeth, and he had to have several extracted. Following one of these surgeries, an infection set in; this led to meningitis. After great suffering he passed away at the age of thirty-two.

When Ivan's death was announced, so deep was the respect he had earned for his total dedication to our Lord and his Church that the bells of Zagreb's cathedral were rung, an honor normally reserved for a bishop. He is the first lay Croat to be a candidate for canonization.

PRAYER

Dear God, through the intercession of Bl. Ivan, help us to persevere and grow in our faith, until we too become inspiring examples of love for you.

Blessed Enrico Rebuschini
April 28, 1860–May 9, 1938
Beatified May 4, 1997

30

Enrico Rebuschini was the second of five children born to a model Christian mother and a father who was what Italians call a *mangia prete*, that is, someone who hates religion. His dad would accompany his family to Mass each Sunday but would wait outside for them.

When Enrico wanted to enter the religious life after high school, his father's staunch opposition prevented him; he entered the University of Pavia to study math instead. He soon left, however, because the anticlericalism at the university made his own father's pale in comparison.

Since Italian men of the time were compelled to complete a period of military service, Enrico entered the Military School of Milan and was eventually commissioned second lieutenant. He was such an exemplary officer that his superiors wanted him to make the military a career, but he chose to study accounting instead.

After graduating at the top of his class, Enrico was hired by his brother-in-law to handle the books for his silk business. Within a few years, however, it was evident from his depression that he could not, as he wrote his brother-in-law, "remain in a path that doesn't suit my nature (and which makes me unhappy)."[1] He could do the job and even liked some of its functions, but he really wanted to become a religious.

His father still vociferously opposed this, but when Enrico's depression increased and caused him to stop eating, his father gave his consent. He could not stand to see his beloved son looking thin and sickly.

Three months later Enrico was studying theology at Rome's famous Gregorian University, where he earned everyone's respect not only for his academic acumen but for his edifying comportment. When his parents came to visit later that year, they saw that he was at last, his mother wrote, "content and at peace."[2]

A year later, however, Enrico's body exchanged the former mental depression for a nervous one. If he had had a stronger constitution, his body might have been able to handle his extreme mortifications, but he was always somewhat weak, and so his body collapsed from lack of proper food and rest. After some time at home and at a spa, his health returned. This experience galvanized the young man's trust in God and his "total confidence in His infinite goodness and mercy."[3]

But by the time Enrico recovered, the school year was effectively done, so he spent the summer working in a hospital at Como. Rather than doing the job assigned to him, he spent nearly all his time at the bedsides of the poor and those who had no one else to comfort them. He believed these "sick Lords" were powerfully close to God precisely because of their suffering, and their care was his first concern. The neglect of his assigned duties led to his dismissal. Nonetheless it was this hospital experience that kindled in him a desire to serve God through the sick.

In September 1887 Enrico went to Verona and there entered

the Camillians, an order dedicated to serving the infirm. He was the old man among the novices. Their youthful vigor irritated him, and he sometimes let his annoyance show by sharp replies to innocent questions. He was told to work on his friendliness, so every day he tried to surrender his antipathy to charity. Little by little he softened up.

Ordained to the priesthood by the future St. Pius X, Fr. Enrico continued to have problems with mental and nervous depression, the latter due in part to the continued mortifications that his frail body could not handle. What saved him was working in a hospital, where he was forced to focus on others and not himself. He also served as a military chaplain, and both patients and soldiers thought him a saint. Indeed, people who would not think of approaching their home priest for the sacraments gladly went to him, because as one person put it, "he had the words and attitudes to convince" them. Depression kept creeping back into his life until 1922, when he kicked the problem for good and was described as "utterly balanced."[4]

Fr. Enrico was made bursar of his community. In addition to his accounting duties, he was the handyman, making electrical and plumbing repairs. He did this job for thirty-five years.

In April 1938, returning home from a sick call, Fr. Enrico came down with a cold. It seemed to be nothing at first but developed into bronchial pneumonia, and he rapidly deteriorated. After requesting forgiveness for any bad example he may have had given and asking that people pray for him, he received Communion. He died several hours later. He was seventy-eight years old.

PRAYER

Dear God, so many of our brothers and sisters are unhappy. Maybe it is because they refuse to accept the path you have laid out for them, but maybe, like Bl. Enrico, it is because they have seen that path and have impediments to following it. Through his prayers, help them to come through their depression with a clear vision of your will and the strength and ability to do it.

Saint Leopold Mandić

May 12, 1866–July 30, 1942

Beatified May 2, 1976

Canonized October 16, 1983

31

Sometimes we have a vision of how we will serve God, and it is a good vision, even a holy vision. But that doesn't mean it is *his* vision.

Leopold Mandić knew this all too well. While he wanted to be a missionary in his native Croatia, he instead spent his entire priestly life in northern Italy. The result, however, was that he became one of the greatest confessors the Church has ever known.

Given the name Bogdan at birth, this twelfth child of a minor Croatian noble family had terrible health. Physical deformities stunted his growth (he was just four feet, five inches tall), he had a funny way of walking, and he stuttered when he spoke. In addition he had chronic arthritis, suffered from regular stomach pains, and couldn't see well.

Some Italian Capuchins were missionaries in his area, and they helped rejuvenate and keep the faith alive there. Aching to follow in their footsteps and evangelize his people, many of whom were not Catholic, Bogdan joined the order at age sixteen, taking the religious name Leopold. He was sent to neighboring Italy for his studies, first to Bassano del Grappa and then to Venice, where he was ordained at age twenty-four.

After ordination Fr. Leopold wanted to return to his native Croatia, but his superiors would not let him because of his frail health. Indeed, because of his weak voice, they wouldn't even let him preach at Mass. When asked his feelings about this once, Leopold replied, "I am like a bird in a cage, but my heart is beyond the seas."[1] Although he could not be where he wanted, his heart and prayers transcended the bonds of time and place.

Thus, with the exception of the year he spent in southern Italy during World War I because of his nationality (Croatia was part of the Austro-Hungarian Empire, Italy's enemy), he ended up living in Padua for the last thirty-six years of his life. He decided to do what he could where he was, and so he spent the vast majority of his day hearing confessions, sometimes fifteen hours at a stretch. Keep in mind that his "confessional" was often his cell, which was bitterly cold in the winter and witheringly hot in the summer.

Fr. Leopold was the object of scorn among his confreres to begin with, and they criticized him even more for being an indulgent confessor. But as Leopold put it, "If you come and kneel before me, isn't this a sufficient proof that you want to have God's pardon? God's mercy is beyond all expectation."[2] He also said, "I give my penitents only small penances because I do the rest myself."[3]

Some believe this lenience grew out of his own experiences as a child when his parents lost all their wealth. Perhaps this experience helped make him extremely sympathetic to the plight of others. This tendency is also apparent in his work on behalf of the sick, poor, and disadvantaged. He had a special heart for the disadvantaged in the womb and spoke out against abortion, establishing orphanages, and treating expectant mothers and their children with great kindness.

Much of this impetus to show the light of Christ and lead others to him came from his deep devotion to Our Lady, whom he called "my holy boss." He was always praying the rosary, and when he celebrated Mass each day, it was at a side altar dedicated to the Blessed Virgin.

Having contracted cancer of the esophagus, Leopold grew progressively weaker, and while preparing to celebrate Mass one morning, he collapsed. He was brought back to his cell to receive the last rites. There the friars gathered to sing the *Salve Regina*, and as they chanted, "O clement, O loving, O sweet Virgin Mary," he breathed his last.

Before his death Fr. Leopold had predicted that his monastery would be bombed, and all would be destroyed except his cell-confessional, since it was a "monument to God's goodness."[4] On May 14, 1944, his prediction came to pass.

PRAYER

Lord, help us remember with St. Leopold that we do not know better than you and that your plans are superior to our own.

For I know the plans I have for you, says the LORD, plans for welfare and not for evil, to give you a future and a hope. (Jeremiah 29:11)

Trust in the LORD with all your heart,
  and do not rely on your own insight.
In all your ways acknowledge him,
  and he will make straight your paths. (Proverbs 3:5–6)

Blessed Maria Restituta Kafka

May 1, 1894–March 30, 1943

Beatified June 21, 1998

32

Most of us are familiar with how putridly evil the Nazis were. Often our impression is that most people living under them either kept quiet or resisted them in secret. There were, however, some brave souls, such as Bl. Maria Restituta Kafka, who were not at all quiet in their opposition.

The sixth daughter of a Czech shoemaker who moved his family to Vienna, Maria was an average student with a terrible stuttering problem, which a teacher solved when he forbade her to speak for three months. She left school at age fifteen and tried her hand at various jobs, including being a maid and a sales clerk in a tobacco shop. She finally decided to become a nurse because she wanted to aid those in need of care and compassion.

Attracted by their piety and way of life, Maria started out as a nursing apprentice in a hospital run by the Franciscan Sisters of Christian Charity. After several months she asked her parents for permission to join the sisters. Her parents refused, and so when she was nineteen and still a minor under the law, Maria ran away from home. Seeing her determination, her parents finally consented, and the congregation accepted her as a postulant, even though she did not have the requisite dowry. Taking the name

Restituta after an early martyr who had been beheaded, she made her final vows in 1918 at age twenty-three, and started working as a full-fledged nurse two years later.

The chief surgeon at her hospital was a humorless, difficult man, and no one wanted to work with him. Sr. Restituta volunteered to do so, however, and within a short time, she was running his operating room. Eventually she became respected as a world-class surgical nurse who fought for the poor.

After the *Anschluss*, the Nazi annexation of Austria, Sr. Restituta protected a Nazi doctor who she thought was about to be unjustly arrested. People started calling her "Sister Resolute," because when she had her mind set, there was no moving her.

Most of the time, however, Sr. Restituta was caring and easygoing, and she had a very good sense of humor. After work she would stop into a local pub and order a bowl of goulash and "a pint of the usual."

Sister was not only resolute but brave, as we see from her very vocal expression of her dislike for the Nazis, who closed her convent and put the hospital under secular control. She even called Hitler a madman. When she hung a crucifix in every room of the hospital's new wing, the Nazis told her to take them down. She refused, and the crucifixes stayed. The only reason the new head doctor, a fanatical Nazi, did nothing was because Sister's skills made her indispensable.

But when anti-Nazi propaganda was discovered in Sister's office, including an anti-Hitler poem in her typewriter, even this doctor would not protect her. She was taken away by the Gestapo on Ash Wednesday 1942. For eight months she subsisted on meager prison rations, but even these she often gave to others who she thought needed them more. This is how she saved the life of a pregnant woman and her children who were in jail with her.

On October 28, 1942, a Nazi tribunal sentenced Sr. Restituta to death for aiding the enemy and plotting treason. Although a wide range of people including Vienna's cardinal asked for clemency, Hitler's private secretary and Nazi Party chief Martin Bormann decided to use her execution as an example. (At one point it seems she was offered her freedom if she would give up religious life, an offer she naturally rejected.)

Sr. Restituta spent the remaining five months of her life ministering to other prisoners. Led to the scaffold wearing only a paper shirt and weighing just half of what she had prior to her arrest, she stopped at the door of the execution chamber and asked the prison chaplain to trace the Sign of the Cross on her forehead. "I have lived for Christ," she said, "I want to die for Christ."[1]

Moments later she lay down before the guillotine and was beheaded. Not wanting her to be revered as a martyr, the Nazis tossed her corpse into a mass grave.

PRAYER

Lord, your servant Bl. Restituta stood up against injustice, untruth, and oppression. While the circumstances differ, we also face these challenges. Through her intercession, help us to find prudent and yet equally fearless means to work for your sake toward a more just world. Give us the ability to echo her final words: "I have lived for Christ; I want to die for Christ."

Blessed Franz Jägerstätter

May 20, 1907–August 9, 1943

Beatified October 26, 2007

33

There were many Catholic heroes among the resisters to the Nazis during their reign of terror, but, and this is saying something, none is as…what? Striking? Admirable? Inspiring? *Compelling* as Franz Jägerstätter.

Franz was born out of wedlock, since his parents were too poor to marry. Indeed, his mother was too poor to raise Franz, so she left him with his deeply pious grandmother, who already had thirteen children to feed, and there was never really enough to eat. Compounding the boy's difficult life, the kids at school picked on Franz because of his poverty and his familial status.

The chances of his parents' marrying ended when his father died in World War I. His mother later married a man named Jägerstätter, who adopted Franz and gave him a home. His step-grandfather had an impressive library, and Franz became an avid reader.

As Franz grew into a teenager, he ran with a gang. He and his friends sometimes drank heavily, and sometimes after drinking they fought, and one source says that when they fought, they fought with weapons. He was also the first in his village to have what was then the ultimate icon of cool and tough, a motorcycle.

He even fathered a daughter (she was ten when he died, and when she learned her daddy had been executed, she was inconsolable).

In the late twenties Franz went to work in some ore mines. His fellow miners delighted in attacking the Catholic faith, and ironically, this led to his conversion. He began attending Mass, and he soon found that the joys of contemplating God—through prayer, the breviary and other spiritual reading, and more prayer—outweighed the fun he experienced with his gang. He even thought about becoming a priest, but this was in the midst of the Depression, and he was his now-widowed mother's lone support. He opted for the lay life.

When Franz eventually returned to his hometown, people immediately saw a change. Around this time he met a young lady named Franziska, and her first question of him was whether he attended Mass. They married not long after and went to Rome for their honeymoon, which amounted to an unheard-of expense, equal to seven months of Franziska's pay.

The real change in Franz came after his marriage. Franziska urged him on to new spiritual heights (which shows just how important it is to marry a good spouse who is as concerned about eternal happiness as about earthly happiness). He was in the process of becoming pious, practicing, and prayerful; she already was.

People are funny. If you are they way Franz used to be, they don't like it, but become "too" religious and they think that is just as bad. In any case, the townspeople saw all this and gave him a hard time, and they blamed Franziska for this "change." But it wasn't as though she forced him to become more devout. Rather, she inspired him. She made him a better man, and he made her a better woman. He once remarked, "I could never have imagined that being married could be so wonderful."[1]

With her encouragement he fasted each day until noonday Mass, and though they were not wealthy by any stretch, they gave what they could to aid the poor.

As World War II commenced, it became dangerous to be anti-Nazi. Franz wasn't at all vocal in his opposition to Nazism, but his position was no secret. He would not donate to Nazi "charities" or vote for the *Anschluss*, the referendum uniting Germany and Austria. These and other actions showed his opposition to be complete, palpable, and undeniable. Because he was not only responsible for his wife and their three daughters but also his widowed mother and his other daughter, his parish priest told him to be careful.

When on Holy Thursday 1938 the Austrian people nearly unanimously voted for *Anschluss*, Franz was the only man in his village to vote against it. He later compared that vote to what happened on the day after the first Holy Thursday, when the people chose Barabbas over the Lord.

A year later the Nazis drafted Franz and assigned him to the motor corps. Twice he received deferments because he was a farmer, and he decided that if called up a third time, he would not serve.

Meanwhile the new parish priest noticed his holiness and asked him to be the sacristan, to which he agreed. When people tried to give him monetary remembrances after funerals and weddings, he would refuse and ask for prayers instead. Franz needed prayer: He couldn't cooperate with the evil of Nazism, but he had to support his family too.

He consulted his parish priest and other priests, even the bishop of Linz. All told him that if he was called back to the army, he should go because his death—and all conscientious objectors were executed—would leave his family without support. His wife and mother said the same thing. The police chief didn't want to arrest him, so he urged Franz to accept a noncombatant role.

The interesting thing is that it wasn't as if he knew from the beginning that he couldn't serve in the *Heer*, the German infantry. He had, after all, already served two short stints. Instead, he gradually came to this realization during his second mobilization. This became cemented through his own observations and letters with friends and relatives who were serving at the front.

Some have tried to say that Franz's eventual decision was a judgment that serving in war, any war, is unjust. However, the eleven questions he prepared for his meeting with the bishop conclusively show that it was *this* war that was in question. Had the war been just, had he not been convinced of the Nazi regime's irredeemable evil and its plan to destroy Christianity after the war, his decision might have been different. His letters show that were it not for the fact that Hitler demanded near religious obeisance to himself, Franz would have felt obliged to be "obedient even unto death."

Furthermore, the appalling numbers of men from his area who were dying at the front led him to believe that if you know you must die, die for something worthy and good. Do not die for evil.

Ultimately Franz decided that God would not let him lie, even for the sake of his family. "I cannot believe that, just because one has a wife and children," he said, "a man is free to offend God. Did not Christ himself say 'He who loves father, mother, or children more than me is not deserving of my kingdom'?"[2]

In February 1943 Franz received the order to report for duty. He told the authorities that while he would serve as a paramedic, he refused to fight. He was immediately arrested and sent to prison in Linz.

The torture and interrogation he experienced there gave him doubts, but his wife kept encouraging him to do what he thought right. He also learned that an Austrian Pallottine priest had suffered the same fate the year before. These factors bolstered him and helped make him resolute. He again offered to serve as a paramedic. The Nazis again refused his offer.

Franz spent some of his incarceration writing highly edifying letters to his wife and godson, and he spent a lot of time praying. "As long as I can pray, my life is not in vain."

His letters show he was not a great fan of the Allies either. He thought both they and the Nazis served pagan ends, albeit in extremely different ways: the Nazis by divorcing man from God and actually promulgating an openly pagan system; the Allies, on the other hand, by seeing man as an end unto himself and serving a system, whether capitalist or communist, that was in no way dedicated to building up the kingdom of God on earth.

The pressure to abandon his principles was almost unrelenting. His parish priest and his understandably conflicted wife made the trip from Austria to Berlin, where he was now imprisoned, to reason with him. His wife even gave him a picture with their daughters holding a sign that said, "Daddy, come home soon!" He told his pastor, "I'm sorry, Your Reverence, but you just haven't been given the grace."[3] Only the prison chaplain unwaveringly supported him.

When the trial finally came, Franz told the court, "This regime is evil, and I cannot support it in any way."[4] His arguments were so persuasive that his accusers went from being imperious and demanding to pleading with him to reconsider.

On the day of his execution, Franz was led to the guillotine. The Nazis made their condemned lie face up and did not blindfold them. The other condemned men were crying, delirious, on the point of insanity, but Franz, prayerful and collected, met his fate calmly. He died at thirty-six years of age, on the same day St. Edith Stein met her end at Auschwitz. His wife and all four daughters were present at his beatification ceremony.[5]

PRAYER

Lord, from the very beginning, humankind has been tempted to believe we can go against conscience for a "good" reason (see Genesis 3:4–5). Help us remember there is no good reason for offending you if prayer and discernment have shown us something is wrong in your eyes. The next time we are pressured into going against the principles you have laid upon our hearts, help us recall Bl. Franz's example and ask for his prayers.

Blessed Nicholas Bunkerd Kitbamrung

February 28, 1895–January 12, 1944

Beatified March 5, 2000

34

Sharing the gospel is rarely if ever a comfortable thing, and it often brings with it both perceived and very real dangers. Sometimes we simply fear being mocked or pegged as "religious zealots" or "Jesus freaks." Sometimes we fear the loss of a job or worse. Evangelization is an essential task, and yet accomplishing it is frightening, isn't it?

Bl. Nicholas Bunkerd Kitbamrung experienced these fears. In conquering them he won many souls for Christ.

Nicholas was the first son of five children born to convert parents near Bangkok, Thailand, at a time when the French ruled nearby Indochina (now Vietnam, Laos, and Cambodia). The French were always attempting to take more Thai land, and they were hated for it. Many saw the Catholic Church as simply a product of the French colonial culture. They didn't judge Christianity on its own merits, so those who became Catholic were looked upon with distrust and suspicion.

Despite the antipathy toward his religion, Nicholas discerned his priestly vocation at a young age and entered the seminary at thirteen. His mother gave her consent only because she thought her young boy would soon be back. But his vocation was genuine, and he received ordination in 1926.

From the start Nicholas was an impressive priest, and his bishop, who had baptized him as an infant, was deeply impressed with his zeal for his priestly duty, considering him his son and the "best priest we had."[1] He sent him to serve as a pastor in northern Vietnam from 1930 to 1937.

While Fr. Nicholas helped all his people, he endeavored in a special way to bring back Catholics who had left the Church due to poverty. (People were offered financial assistance if they would apostatize.) He once took money that had been given him to replace his worn and tattered cassock and gave it to the poor. Fr. Nicholas's friendly, genial manner also helped him get permission to preach in Buddhist temples, and converts occasionally came from these encounters.

Later he returned to his native land. During the French-Thai War (1940–1941), the suspicion under which all Catholics fell blossomed, and Fr. Nicholas was accused of spying for and collaborating with the French. Arrested on Sunday, January 12, 1941, he spent nine months awaiting trial. He was eventually convicted because of the testimony of false witnesses, and the judge sentenced him to fifteen years in prison.

The imprisoned Fr. Nicholas experienced torture and bad conditions, and these led to tuberculosis, but he never stopped trying to evangelize his fellow prisoners. Possibly the greatest catechism lesson he taught them was the love, endurance, and perseverance he demonstrated. During his time in jail, he baptized sixty-eight men.

Tuberculosis was typically deadly at the time, and Fr. Nicholas lacked proper care. He died three years to the day after being arrested.

PRAYER

Lord, help us remember that even though being a Christian is often an unpopular calling, you don't call us to be popular. "You will be hated by all for my name's sake," you told us, "but he who endures to the end will be saved" (Mark 13:13). Since sharing our faith can be uncomfortable, since it can even make us hated, help us to remember the courage and example of Bl. Nicholas, who spread our holy religion in ways large and small. With his prayers, help us bring souls to you.

Blessed Claudio Granzotto
August 23, 1900–August 15, 1947
Beatified November 20, 1994

35

Sometimes we're tempted to think we don't have anything special to offer God. We're not smart, or we don't speak very well, or we have trouble praying. We can't be saints because we're not like those "holy" people.

But the life of Claudio Granzotto shows that our Lord has given each of us some special ability, however modest it may be. And rather than bury these talents in the sand, we can use them for his greater glory.

Given the name Riccardo at his birth in Santa Lucia del Piave near Venice, he was the youngest of nine children from a peasant farming family. His father died when he was only nine years old, and to help keep his family fed, Riccardo had to learn many skills besides farming, such as carpentry, bricklaying, and even shoe-making. His passion, however, was always art.

After serving in the army and working several jobs, Riccardo finally achieved his dream of entering the Academy of Fine Arts in Venice in 1922. Often going without food in order to afford tuition and supplies, and overcoming numerous other difficulties as well, he graduated after seven years with honors as a "professor of sculpture."

Riccardo quickly began attracting attention, and in 1930 he won a competition to sculpt a statue of a ballplayer to be placed in the Foro Mussolini in Rome. He ultimately declined the commission, however, because he did not want to meet the prerequisite, which was to join the Fascist party.

Riccardo Granzotto's work shows the most exquisite mastery of the human body. One piece he did after entering religious life that shows this in a particular way portrays Christ in the tomb, which he began after making a pilgrimage to the Shroud of Turin. Almost all his art demonstrates some aspect of his faith, such as his special devotion to the Blessed Mother, for whom he built a copy of the Lourdes grotto in Chiampo, Italy.

Indeed, Riccardo's life of prayer and fidelity to the faith was the primary inspiration not only for his art but for his entire life. He took whatever opportunity he could to pray in front of the tabernacle, even if he could only spare a few moments, "because," as he told his pastor, "if Jesus is there, where else would you want to be?"[1]

He wrote, "The Eucharist is the source of true peace. How much joy would Jesus have from priests, religious, and the faithful if they spent more time before the tabernacle in adoration! … What divine power men would have to love God."[2]

Although he was becoming known as a promising artist and earning increasingly larger commissions, at some point Riccardo felt the pull of Jesus. He entered the Franciscans as a brother in 1933, taking the name Claudio. His pastor wrote, "The Order is receiving not only an artist but a saint."[3]

Truth be told, one could say that Claudio's greatest artistic endeavor was to sculpt himself as an image of abandonment to Divine Providence. He utterly surrendered himself to God's will, and this union was so complete that he was known to have mystical visions. When a confrere asked him, "How many books must I read to discover the secret of your prayer?" Fra Claudio replied, "One book alone: the Crucifix."[4]

Given that he was a Franciscan, it should not be surprising that he had a special concern for the poor and sick, for whom he sacrificed his own food during the war. Even though he was famous, he had extraordinary humility, and he absolutely loved the virtue of chastity. For these and many other reasons, the friar who wanted to "remain hidden like a grain of sand"[5] saw the fame of his holiness spread.

Sadly, this man with the amazingly creative mind developed brain cancer and kept it hidden until it was too late. When his fellow friars finally discovered it, they rushed him to the hospital in a desperate attempt to save him. When they arrived, however, the doctor yelled, "You have brought me a dead man!"[6]

Claudio died at dawn on the Feast of the Assumption in 1947, as the Virgin had predicted to him in a dream.

PRAYER

Father God, you have blessed each of your children with unique talents, for which we praise your holy name. Through the inspiration of Bl. Claudio, help us use our gifts for our sanctification, the increase of Holy Mother Church, and your greater glory.

Blessed Luigi and Maria Beltrame Quattrocchi

January 12, 1880–November 9, 1951 and
June 24, 1884–August 25, 1965
Beatified October 21, 2001

36

37

With a 50-percent divorce rate and the carnage of broken families all around us, our world needs stout models of marital fidelity and holiness as a sort of compass to keep us on course. We are blessed to have one in the Church's first beatified couple, Luigi and Maria Beltrame Quattrocchi. Theirs is an ideal few can reach, frankly, but oh, what an ideal.

Although Luigi was born in Sicily, his parents sent him to live with his childless aunt and uncle. So while he stayed in touch with his parents and siblings, this pair raised him. In deference to this fact, he added their surname, Quattrocchi.

Luigi moved with his aunt and uncle to Rome in 1892. Ten years later he graduated from law school, and shortly thereafter he earned a faculty position at Sapienza University, where his legal scholarship won him great respect.

Maria was born in Florence to a noble family that often moved because of her father's military service, which is why they moved to Rome in 1893. A good student, she obtained a license in teaching and later became a professor of education and the author of several books.

Her parents became friends with the Quattrocchis, which is how Luigi and Maria met. After a five-year courtship, the two married on November 25, 1905, at the Basilica of St. Mary Major in Rome.

Until he met Maria, Luigi was not terribly devout, but she helped him see the joy of faith. Working together, as their son later wrote, there "was a kind of race between" them to grow in holiness.

To help them toward this goal, Maria placed herself under the spiritual direction of the famous Dominican theologian Dom Reginald Garrigou-Lagrange, and each month the couple made a retreat under the direction of Bl. Ildefonso Schuster. They also took graduate religion courses at the Pontifical Gregorian University. Additionally, the Beltrame Quattrocchis annually consecrated their home to the Sacred Heart, and they observed First Fridays. Perhaps most importantly, both put the other's happiness before their own. Maria wrote:

> The day started with Mass and Communion together. When we left the church [the same one in which they had married], he said hello to me as if that was when the day started. We bought a newspaper on the way home, and then he went off to his work and me to my occupations. But always, we thought unceasingly of one another. With what joy did I wait for his key to turn the lock in the door, and each time I thought it was him, I blessed the Lord with all my heart! We then had several quiet conversations, which were both merry and mischievous, speaking a little about many things. ... His remarks were always wise. He was always kind....

> We had in common ... the same aspirations and goals,
> a great support for one another, and an immense love.
> Each moment of conversation, each exchange, every
> attention we gave one another, each touch, had the savor
> of newness. During almost 50 years of married life, I
> affirm before God that we never knew a moment of trou-
> ble, satiety, or boredom.[1]

Their daughter implicitly confirms this. "It is obvious to think that at times they had differences of opinion, but we, their children, were never exposed to these. They solved their problems between themselves through conversation, so that once they came to an agreement, the atmosphere continued to be serene."[2]

As in most marriages, the couple faced financial pressures. After all, they lived through two world wars and the Great Depression in a quasi-socialist country. However, they took such circumstances of life and sanctified them through prayer, offering them up and trying to approach them as Jesus would.

Maria and Luigi assisted anyone who came to them for help, mostly with money or food but sometimes with just a willing ear, a kind word, and a smile when that was all they could afford to give. Their home was a house of faith and all that means.

During World War II they refused to take part in anything having to do with fascism, and they hid Jews. After the war Luigi filled many governmental posts to help in Italy's reconstruction effort, and for his labors the government made him deputy attorney general. For her part Maria devoted herself to raising the family and later became the caregiver for Luigi's aged parents.

As might be expected, the couple raised their children to be devout, practicing Catholics, reciting the rosary each day and also ensuring that there was a lot of joy in their home. Luigi and Maria constantly sought a healthy balance between prayer, work, and leisure. They took walks together and opened their children's minds to the arts and culture. On holidays they took the children to the beach and to the mountains. And like a lot of dads, Luigi taught his boys how to play sports.

After conceiving their fourth child, Maria had a very difficult pregnancy, in which her chances of survival were just 5 percent. The doctors recommended the Beltrame Quattrocchis abort the child, which they of course refused, and their daughter was born without any complications.

Nonetheless the couple couldn't risk another pregnancy. Back then people didn't know about Natural Family Planning, and the only option for good Catholics was to abstain. So after twenty-one years of marriage, the couple renounced their recourse to the marriage bed. This was, their children related, a "difficult vow" for them, but for twenty years they lovingly offered up this valued part of their married life as a sacrifice for the kingdom, in the spirit of Colossians 1:24.

Luigi passed away from a heart attack. His wife lived another fourteen years, leaving this world in her youngest daughter's arms at her house in the mountains. Of their four children, two became priests, and their oldest daughter became a nun (she was the only one of their offspring who didn't live to see their beatification ceremony). Their feast is celebrated on the day of their marriage.

A Web site has been established to post requests for the Beltrame Quattrocchis' intercession on behalf of troubled marriages. The address is http://anashford.tripod.com.

PRAYER

Jesus, you gave us marriage as an indissoluble sacrament for the pro-creation and education of children and for the spouses' mutual assistance to heaven. Furthermore, in the Beltrame Quattrocchis you gave us an incredible example of how this can all be joyfully and lovingly accomplished. We ask that through their example and their prayers, you would repair broken marriages, heal troubled marriages, and greatly strengthen good marriages. Show all couples that marriage can be a thing of joy and beauty and a shining image of the loving relationship you desire with each one of us.

Saint Gaetano Catanoso

February 14, 1879–April 4, 1963

Beatified May 4, 1997

Canonized October 23, 2005

38

If there were a Hall of Fame for priests, Don Gaetano (also known as Cajetan) Catanoso would have his own wing.

The eighth of ten children born to parents who were wealthy, devout landowners in southern Italy, Gaetano always knew he wanted to be a priest. As a result, he entered the minor seminary at age ten. Two years after his ordination to the priesthood in 1902, at the age of twenty-three, he was assigned to a parish in rural and isolated Pentidatillo, where he stayed until 1921.

During his tenure at Pentidatillo, Fr. Gaetano developed a profound devotion to the Holy Face. This grew out of his unremitting attempt to see the face of Jesus in everyone, especially the suffering. After all, he saw much suffering in this rural area, where farmers struggled to produce food, orphans had no one to care for them, and people lived without basic necessities. Because of this overwhelming poverty and the attendant illiteracy, the Mafia tantalized many, and so his community was wracked by crime.

"The Holy Face is my life," he wrote. "He is my strength."[1] Fueled by this dedication, Fr. Gaetano started evening schools for children in the hopes that education would give them different opportunities.

In 1921 the bishop transferred Fr. Gaetano to the large parish of Santa Maria de la Candelaria in urban Reggio di Calabria, where he served until 1940. From this more affluent parish he was able to help provide poorer churches with funds for restoration. He never tired of trying to make his parishioners comprehend that, as members of the universal Church, they were part of a larger reality.

Fr. Gaetano also stressed with his parishioners the importance of their personal catechesis of their children and of keeping Sundays and feast days holy. In addition to promoting devotion to the Holy Face, he initiated Marian devotions and Eucharistic Adoration, and during these events he would have a phalanx of priests on hand to hear confessions. None of this is surprising from a priest who himself spent long hours before the Blessed Sacrament and who had an unusually strong sense of sin and humankind's need for divine mercy.

While Father's parents had been able to afford his seminary education, he realized there were many who could not do the same for their sons. Not wanting any worthy man to be denied the priesthood simply because of lack of resources, he started a scholarship fund. Following the war his area was inundated with orphans, so he founded an orphanage.

He also founded a religious congregation, the Veronican Sisters of the Holy Face, which ran schools and homes for the elderly. When for some reason the archbishop suppressed this good and holy work, Father submitted to His Excellency's order with great humility and obedience. The congregation was eventually approved.

Indeed, Fr. Gaetano never lacked for something to do. In addition to his other pastoral activities, he served as confessor to a prison and several religious institutes, as a hospital chaplain, and as the spiritual director at the local seminary.

With age came illness and blindness. St. Gaetano spent his last years at the motherhouse of the Veronican Sisters, where he provided spiritual direction and heard confessions. He died at eighty-four years of age.

PRAYER

Father, you know our painful shortage of priests. The harvest is potentially great, but the laborers are few. Please send us tireless, fearless men such as St. Gaetano so that souls may have shepherds who will teach them their true worth and ultimate destiny. And through his prayers and example, may our current priests be encouraged to grow in both their efforts and their holiness.

Saint Pio Forgione of Pietrelcina

May 25, 1887–September 23, 1968
Beatified May 2, 1999
Canonized June 16, 2002

39

Anyone taking an objective look at the last hundred or so years can see that this period has witnessed a tsunami of sin. Things that were once unthinkable became not only tacitly accepted but actively championed. However, as St. Paul writes, "Where sin increased, grace abounded all the more" (Romans 5:20), and outside of Our Lady and St. Joseph, there is no greater example of this in human form than Padre Pio.

Born Francesco Forgione in the small farming town of Pietrelcina, Italy, he was singularly touched by grace from a very early age. By the age of five he had already decided to commit his entire life to our Lord. This is also when he began practicing corporal mortifications, such as sleeping on the floor with a stone for a pillow, much as St. Francis had done.

Pietrelcina was a highly religious village, where people regularly celebrated saints' feast days and tried in other ways to imbue daily life with the sensibility of faith. In this respect the Forgione family were regular townsfolk. Their daily Mass attendance, nightly rosary, and three-days-per-week abstention from meat in honor of Our Lady of Mount Carmel were not unusual. Though his grandparents could not read, they memorized Scripture passages and would recite these to their children and grandchildren. All of this contributed to Francesco's decision to follow Christ in the priesthood.

Of course, the fact that he had visions of Jesus, Mary, and his guardian angel and regularly fell into ecstasy probably had something to with this decision as well. The only question remaining was, what direction would his call to the priesthood take?

That question was answered for him at around age thirteen, when a Capuchin friar came to town seeking alms. Francesco was captivated by this order's charism. He made a visit with his parents to the nearest friary, but the friars rejected him because he didn't have enough education. In the late nineteenth century, schooling was not as high a priority for many farming families as having hands in the field.

To earn enough money to afford a tutor for his son, Francesco's father went to work in the United States. The tutoring enabled the boy to catch up in school, and in 1903, at age fifteen, he entered the novitiate at Morcone, taking the name Pio in honor of Pietrelcina's patron saint, Pius V.

Ordained to the priesthood in 1910, Padre Pio spent his next six years with his family due to his poor health. After his return to the monastery, his superiors sent him to the remote mountain town of San Giovanni Rotondo. Except for a six-month stint as a medic during World War I (military service was compulsory even for priests, though Pio was an invalid for most of this period), this is where he spent the rest of his life.

After his return from the army, Padre Pio spent much of his time providing spiritual direction for the many people who knew his reputation for sanctity and wanted to become saints themselves. For his directees he counseled five things: weekly confession, daily Communion, daily spiritual reading, twice daily meditation on that reading, and a twice daily examination of conscience, once at midmorning and again in the evening. He compared weekly confession to cleaning the house, and his steady counsel was to seek the will of God in all things and then to "pray, hope, and don't worry."[1]

Padre Pio lived what he preached. He endured much by the Lord's grace, and with great patience and trust on his part. His whole life he suffered from terrible illnesses. He had to trust that God would enable him to become educated enough to enter the novitiate. And then there were violent attacks from Satan, some of which made St. Pio feel as if he were in the depths of hell.

Satan would either physically assault Pio or, in an effort to lead him astray, appear as various persons, such as his provincial. Over time he learned to tell between a vision from God and a false apparition by discerning his state of mind and the feelings the vision left in him. If he felt peace and calm at first but disturbed afterward, he knew the vision was false. If he felt fearful at first but joyful and at peace later, he knew it was legitimate.

The spiritual phenomenon for which Padre Pio was most known was the stigmata. He was the only man after St. Francis to experience these visible signs of Christ's sufferings. Pictures often show him in brown gloves, which he wore to hide the blood that seeped from the wounds through the bandages. The wounds were painful, and he felt them not only on his hands, on his feet, and in his side but also, as was recently revealed, on his shoulder, where Christ carried the cross. Many people claimed that the stigmata were self-inflicted or mere psychological manifestations, but extensive investigations by physicians said otherwise.

Padre Pio experienced other supernatural phenomena, such as the aforementioned ecstasy, levitation, prophecy, the ability to read souls, the ability to heal, and the odor of sanctity (a strong flowery scent emanating from the body, especially from the stigmata). He survived for weeks at a time on nothing but the Eucharist. Even when he did eat regular food, he never consumed more than five hundred calories a day.

Pio also had the gift of tongues (see Acts 2:5–12). A woman might come into the confessional speaking, say, Chinese, and he would understand her perfectly. She would likewise understand his Italian.

Another remarkable and mysterious gift was that of bilocation, being in two places at once. People claimed to meet him in Rome while he was also in San Giovanni Rotondo. During World War II a British air crew was on its way to a bombing mission on Nazi positions in Italy. The Nazis, however, had learned of this and were waiting in ambush. The entire British crew reported seeing a Capuchin friar in the sky motioning them to turn around. They did, and when shown a picture of Padre Pio after the war, they confirmed that he was the one they had seen.

There are hundreds of examples of Pio's gift of prophecy. During the war, for instance, soldiers' relatives would show him pictures of loved ones from whom they had not heard. He would tell them whether they were dead, wounded, or simply prisoners. His friend Maria Pyle asked what she would do when he died. "You are going to greet me," he told her.[2] And indeed, she died before he did.

Because of all these spiritual phenomena, thousands flocked each year to see Padre Pio and confess to him. Some days the crowds were so large that he had only three hours of sleep. Still he rose early every morning to say Mass at 5:00 AM.

Padre Pio had periods of profound spiritual unrest, a dark night of the soul in which he, like Mother Teresa after him, felt utterly abandoned by God. He could echo our Lord's words, "My God, my God, why have you forsaken me?" (Matthew 27:46; Mark 15:34; see Psalm 22:1).

Perhaps he felt this way too when, out of honest suspicion or petty jealousy, people accused him of being a fraud, charges that even went to the Holy Office (today known as the Congregation for the Doctrine of the Faith). People claimed that he used acid to inflict the stigmata and cologne to mimic the odor of sanctity. They also accused him of breaking his vows of poverty, chastity, and obedience.

At one point St. Pio was ordered to stop celebrating the sacraments publicly. These commands came from his archbishop, who was no one's idea of a saint. Under Archbishop Gagliardi's censure, Padre Pio was stripped of all priestly faculties except celebration of Mass in his friary's inner chapel. Although shattered, he submitted with what his friend Fr. Agostino recalled as "holy resignation." "God's will be done," Pio is quoted as saying. "The will of the authorities is the will of God." [3]

> Padre Agostino Daniele, Pio's best friend and confessor for more than fifty years, charged that Gagliardi waged "a veritable satanic war" against Padre Pio, soliciting letters with "accusations, exaggerations, and calumnies" to forward to the Vatican—while it was the archbishop himself who was the center of controversy.
>
> So bad was the situation that a number of priests in the archdiocese petitioned Pope Pius XI to end what

they saw as the "disorder," "immorality," and "clerical degeneracy."

... Padre Pio...never retaliated against the archbishop, nor even criticized him. In fact the angriest the famous mystical priest was seen to get was with a supporter—a Pio defender—who had attacked the archbishop.[4]

It was not only the questionable archbishop who restricted the scope of Pio's priesthood but also the Holy Office. This happened in 1922, when he was ordered not to bless crowds or display or even discuss his stigmata. Correspondence was severely restricted, and he was not allowed to see his spiritual director. When someone expressed disgust over Rome's restrictions, St. Pio replied, "You did a wicked thing.... We must respect the decrees of the Church. We must be silent and suffer."[5]

This respect for and fealty to the Church's authority was evident throughout his life. In later years he was quite aware of those who did not like Vatican II and the changes many falsely wrought in its name. His sister left her religious order because she opposed innovations her superiors enacted after the council. While admitting that her charges had merit, he remonstrated with her for her disobedience. "[Your superiors] are wrong and you are right, but still you must obey," he told her. "You must return."[6]

By 1933 Pope Pius XI realized he had been "badly informed" concerning the case against St. Pio, and he not only lifted the ban on his public celebration of the sacraments but also gave him the license to preach, something for which he was not technically qualified. Pius XII actually encouraged people to go to him, and while Bl. John XXIII was ambivalent, Paul VI essentially let it be known that the saint was above all suspicion.

Pio, in turn, supported Pope Paul. A week before Pio died, he wrote His Holiness, "I wish to thank you for the clear and decisive words you pronounce, especially in the last encyclical, *Humanae Vitae*, and I once more affirm my faith and unconditional obedience to your illuminated orders."[7]

Worn out by years of intense pastoral activity and sickness, Padre Pio took ill one last time and died in September 1968. But he had assured people on many occasions, "After my death I will do more. My real mission will begin after my death."[8]

In March 2008 Padre Pio's body was exhumed so as to move it to a better place for veneration. At that time he was found to be well-preserved although not incorrupt.

PRAYER

Lord, you in your ineffable mercy sometimes give us signs to show your great love for us. Padre Pio was such a sign, and we thank you for demonstrating for us just what love for and total dedication to you can accomplish. Through his example help us to draw closer to you, and through his prayers may we be sanctified.

Notes

Introduction

1. Kurt Klinger, ed., *A Pope Laughs: Stories of John XXIII*, Sally McDevitt Cunneen, trans. (New York: Holt, Rinehart, and Winston, 1964), p. 124.

Bl. Mother Teresa of Kolkata and Bl. Mother Mariam Thresia Chiramel Mankidiyan

1. Carol Zaleski, "The Dark Night of Mother Teresa," *First Things*, May 2003, available at www.firstthings.com.

Bl. Jakob Gapp

1. Josef Levit, *Blessed Jacob Gapp, Marianist* (Dayton, Ohio: North American Center for Marianist Studies, 1998), excerpt available at http://www.nacms.org.
2. Levit.
3. Levit.

Bl. Ignatius Maloyan

1. Abdel Ahad Madfuni, "The Great Martyr and Bishop Ignatius Maloyan," Christine Bedros, trans., available at www.armenian-catholic.ru.
2. Dom Antoine Marie, "Blessed Ignatius Maloyan," Letter of St. Joseph Abbey, available at www.clairval.com.
3. Antoine Marie.

Bl. Alberto Marvelli

1. Biography of Alberto Marvelli, available at www.vatican.va.
2. Salesians of Don Bosco UK, "Blessed Alberto Marvelli (1918–1946)," available at www.salesians.org.uk.
3. Don Fausto Lanfranchi quoted these words of Bl. Alberto in correspondence with the author.
4. Lanfranchi.

5. Salesians of Don Bosco.
6. Salesians of Don Bosco.

Bl. Eurosia "Mamma Rosa" Fabris
1. Biography of Eurosia Fabris, available at www.vatican.va.
2. Eurosia Fabris biography, available at http://en.wikipedia.org.
3. "A Great Example of Christian Living," available at http://catholic-newsgeek.blogspot.com.

Bl. Vicente Vilar David
1. "Biographies of New Blesseds–1995," available at www.ewtn.com.
2. Paraphrase of quote in JClub biography of Bl. Vicente David Vilar, available at www.jclubcatholic.org.

Bl. Louis and Zélie Martin
1. "Parents of St. Thérèse," available at www.sttherese.com.
2. "Parents of St. Thérèse."
3. "Parents of St. Thérèse."
4. "Parents of St. Thérèse."
5. Catholic Truth Society pamphlet, "Louis and Zélie Martin, Parents of Thérèse of Lisieux," quoted at http://the-hermeneutic-of-continuity.blogspot.com.
6. "Parents of St. Thérèse."
7. "Her Parents: The Beatification of Louis and Zelie Martin," available at www.littleflower.org.
8. "Her Parents."
9. "Her Parents."
10. "Béatification Louis et Zélie Martin," available at www.carmel.asso.fr, translated by the author.
11. The Church teaches we can not only unite our sufferings with the cross and thus participate in the economy of salvation but also, with the proper direction from competent spiritual authorities, offer ourselves as victims for this purpose. For more on this see the *Catechism of the Catholic Church,* #307, #618, and #1508.

12. "Parents of St. Thérèse."

St. Crispin of Viterbo

1. "St. Crispin of Viterbo, OFM Cap.," available at www.beafriar.com.
2. Plinio Corrêa de Oliveira, "St. Crispin of Viterbo, May 21," available at www.traditioninaction.org.
3. De Oliveira.
4. "Blessed Crispin of Viterbo," *Catholic Encyclopedia,* available at www.newadvent.org.
5. De Oliveira.
6. Capuchin Franciscan Friars of Australia, "Capuchin Saint: Saint Crispin of Viterbo," available at www.capuchinfriars.org.au.

St. Gianna Beretta Molla

1. "Resolutions: Wisdom from Our Patroness," available at http://saint-giannahome.org.
2. "Resolutions."
3. Gianna Beretta Molla, at a Catholic Action Conference, October 21, 1946, available at www.childrenofmedjugorje.com.
4. Molla, Catholic Action Conference.
5. "St. Gianna Beretta Molla—Pro Life—Pro Love," available at www.youtube.com.
6. Helen Hitchcock, "Saint Gianna: A Model for Mothers," introduction to Pietro Molla, Elio Guerriero, and James G. Colbert, *Saint. Gianna Molla: Wife, Mother, Doctor* (San Francisco: Ignatius, 2004).
7. "St. Gianna Beretta Molla—Pro Life—Pro Love."
8. Tom Rosica, "Saint Gianna Beretta Molla," *Catholic Insight,* June 2004, available at www.catholicinsight.com.
9. "St. Gianna Beretta Molla—Pro Life—Pro Love."
10. "St. Gianna Beretta Molla—Pro Life—Pro Love."
11. "Blessed Gianna Beretta Molla," available at www.savior.org.
12. "St. Gianna Beretta Molla—Pro Life—Pro Love."

Bl. Elisabetta Canori Mora

1. Dom Antoine Marie, "Blessed Elisabetta Mora," *Letter of St. Joseph Abbey*, available at www.clairval.com.
2. Antoine Marie.
3. Antoine Marie.
4. Pope John Paul II, Homily for the Eucharistic Concelebration for the Beatification of Isidore Bakanja, Gianna Beretta Molla and Elisabetta Canori Mora, April 24, 1994, available at www.vatican.va.

Bl. Isidore Bakanja

1. "Blessed Isidore Bakanja," available at www.savior.org.
2. "Blessed Isidore Bakanja."
3. "Blessed Isidore Bakanja."
4. Irondequoit Catholic Communities, "Blessed Isidore Bakanja, Martyr," available at www.irondequoitcatholic.org.

St. Josephine Bakhita

1. John Bartunek, "February 8—St. Josephine Bakhita," available at http://catholic.net.
2. Bartunek.
3. Bartunek.
4. "St. Josephine Bakhita, Patron St. of the Canossian Society of the Sacred Heart of Jesus Catholic Church of Whiteville, N.C.," available at http://bcrcatholics.org.
5. Biography of Josephine Bakhita, available at www.vatican.va.

Bl. Pope Pius IX

1. Edgardo Levi-Mortara's Testimony for Beatification of Pius IX, available at www.catholic-forum.com.
2. John Gilmary Shea, *The Life of Pope Pius IX and the Great Events in the History of the Church* (New York: Thomas Kelly, 1877), p. 191.
3. "His Holiness Pope Venerable Pius IX," available at www.pius-theninth.com.

Bl. Marie of Jesus Crucified
1. "Mariam the Little Arab," available at www.katolik.nu.
2. Doris C. Neger, "The Little Arab," *Sophia*, vol. 31, no. 1 (January–February 2001), reprinted at www.melkite.org.
3. Neger.
4. Neger.
5. Correspondence with the author from Sr. Anne-Françoise, postulator of Bl. Marie of Jesus Crucified's canonization cause.
6. Sr. Anne-Françoise.
7. Carmelites of the Holy Land, "Blessed Mary of Jesus Crucified: The Life," available at www.carmelholyland.org.
8. Neger.

Bl. Marie-Joseph Cassant
1. Dom Antoine Marie, "Blessed Marie-Joseph Cassant, O.C.S.O., Monk," available at www.clerus.org.
2. Biography of Joseph-Marie Cassant, available at www.vatican.va.
3. Fr. Mark, "Blessed Joseph-Marie Cassant," Vultus Christi, available at http://vultus.stblogs.org.
4. Antoine Marie.
5. Antoine Marie.
6. Dom Donald, Abbot Emeritus of Nunraw, Scotland, "A Cistercian Menology: Blessed Marie-Joseph Cassant 1878–1903," available at http://nunraw.blogspot.com.
7. See Bl. Marie-Joseph's biography, available at www.ocso.org.
8. Antoine Marie.

St. Agostina Livia Pietrantoni
1. Biography of Agostina Livia Pietrantoni, available at www.vatican.va.
2. Ann Ball, *Modern Saints: Their Lives and Faces, Book One* (Rockford, Ill.: Tan, 2009), p. 128.
3. Biography, www.vatican.va.
4. Biography, www.vatican.va.

5. "Questi uomini non sono cattivi, sono soltanto ammalati. Quanto mi conforta il pensiero che in essi servo Gesù Cristo," available at www.paginecattoliche.it, translated by the author.

6. Biography, available at www.vatican.va.

7. "Suor Agostina, perdona il suo uccisore?" available at www.paginecattoliche.it, translated by the author.

8. Testimony of Mrs. A. Mattogno: "Il martire è colui che scrive le cose di Dio con il suo sangue," available at www. paginecattoliche.it, translated by the author.

Bl. Emperor Karl I

1. Princess Zita, as quoted in Giovanna Brizi, "The Religious Life of Emperor Karl: A Study of the Documents for the Beatification Process," available at http://emperorcharles.org.

2. Brizi.

3. Correspondence with the author from Br. Nathan Cochran, O.S.B., delegate to promote the cause of canonization of Bl. Karl in the United States and Canada.

4. "Charles I of Austria," available at http://en.wikipedia.org.

5. "Charles I of Austria."

6. Pope John Paul II, Homily for the Beatification of Five Servants of God, no. 6, October 3, 2004, available at www.vatican.va.

Bl. Edward Poppe

1. Center for Applied Research in the Apostolate (CARA), "Sacraments Today: Belief and Practice Among U.S. Catholics: Executive Summary," p. 4, available at http://cara.georgetown.edu.

2. Vatican II, *Lumen Gentium*, 11.

3. Dom Antoine Marie, *Letter of St. Joseph Abbey,* May 13, 2001, available at www.clairval.com.

4. Dom Antoine Marie, "Blessed Edward Poppe, Parish Associate Pastor (1890 – 1924 Belgium)," available at www.clerus.org.

5. Antoine Marie, "Blessed Edward Poppe."

6. Antoine Marie, *Letter*.

7. Antoine Marie, *Letter*.

8. Antoine Marie, *Letter*.

9. Antoine Marie, *Letter*.

10. Antoine Marie, *Letter*.

11. Antoine Marie, *Letter*.

Bl. Anna Schäffer

1. Correspondence of Domvikar Georg Schwager with the author.

2. Correspondence of Domvikar Georg Schwager with the author.

Bl. Pina Suriano

1. Biography of Pina Suriano, available at www.vatican.va.

2. Biography.

3. Homily of John Paul II on the Occasion of Bl. Pina's Beatification, no. 6, September 4, 2004, available at www.vatican.va.

4. Delia Gallagher, "History of the Holy House of Loreto, New Saints for the Church," Zenit.org, September 3, 2004, available at www.ewtn.com.

Bl. Bartolo Longo

1. Fr. Daniels, "The Conversion of Blessed Bartolo Longo or the Story of Our Lady of the Rosary of Pompeii," available at www.saintmichael-archangel.com.

Bl. José Luis Sánchez del Río

1. "Biografía de José Luis Sánchez del Río," November 23, 2005, available at www.regnumchristi.org, translated by the author.

2. "José Sánchez del Río," available at http://en.wikipedia.org.

3. "José Sánchez del Río."

Bl. Ivan Merz

1. "Blessed Ivan Merz, Banja Luka, Dec. 16, 1896—Zagreb, May 10, 1928, A 'European-Sized' Apostle of the Youth," available at www.ivanmerz.hr.

2. "Blessed Ivan Merz."
3. "Blessed Ivan Merz."
4. "Blessed Ivan Merz."
5. Correspondence with the author from Fr. Bozidar Nagy, postulator of Bl. Ivan Merz's canonization cause.
6. Nagy.
7. Nagy.

Bl. Enrico Rebuschini
1. Dom Antoine Marie, "Blessed Enrico Rebuschini, Camillian (1860 Como–1938 Cremona)," available at www.clerus.org.
2. Antoine Marie.
3. Antoine Marie.
4. Antoine Marie.

St. Leopold Mandiç
1. Catholic Fire, "Saint of the Day: St. Leopold Bogdan Mandiç," July 28, 2008, available at http://catholicfire.blogspot.com.
2. "Leopold Mandic," May 11, 2009, available at http://breathingwithbothlungs.blogspot.com.
3. "Leopold Mandic."
4. "Capuchin Saint: St. Leopold Mandic, OFM Cap," available at www.beafriar.com.

Bl. Maria Restituta Kafka
1. Alfred de Manche, "Blessed Restituta Kafka, Martyred by the Nazis for the Cross of Christ!" available at http://jerome2007.tripod.com.

Bl. Franz Jägerstätter
1. "Franz Jägerstätter 1907–1943, Martyr: Short Biography," available at http://www.dioezese-linz.at.
2. "Franz Jaegerstaetter," available at www.justpeace.org.
3. "Franz Jaegerstaetter."
4. "Franz Jaegerstaetter."

5. The primary source for this chapter was Erna Putz, *Franz Jägerstätter—Martyr. A Shining Example in Dark Times* (Linz: Catholic Church in Austria, 2007), available at www.dioezese-linz.at.

Bl. Nicholas Bunkerd Kitbamrung

1. "Fr. Nicholas Bridges East to West," available at http://www.fides.org.

Bl. Claudio Granzotto

1. "'Il Serafino dell'Eucarestia': Claudio Granzotto," www.collevalenza.it, translated by the author.
2. "Il Serafino dell'Eucarestia."
3. "Saint of the Day: Blessed Claudio Granzotto," March 23, www.americancatholic.org.
4. "Il Serafino dell'Eucarestia."
5. Archives of Friars Minor, "Dai 'Manoscritti' del beato Claudio Granzotto, religioso," available at www.fraclaudio.it, translated by the author.
6. "Frà Claudio (il Beato Claudio Granzotto, Scultore Veneto, Grande Francescano)," available at www.wikio.it, translated by the author.

Bl. Luigi and Maria Beltrame Quattrocchi

1. "Testimoni Dell'Amore," *Meg Responsabili*, no. 13 (May 19, 2008), available at www.meg-italia.it, translated by the author.
2. Mary Ann Sullivan, "Heroic in Marriage," *Marian Helper*, Spring 2002, available at www.marian.org.

St. Gaetano Catanoso

1. Biography of Gaetano Catanoso, available at www.vatican.va.

St. Pio Forgione of Pietrelcina

1. "Padre Pio: The Man," available at www.ewtn.com.
2. "Saint Pio of Pietrelcina: The Gift of Prophecy," available at www.catholictradition.org.
3. "Padre Pio's Response to a 'Wayward' Bishop," *Spirit Daily*, reprinted at www.catholicity.com.

4. "Padre Pio's Response."

5. "Padre Pio's Response."

6. "Padre Pio's Response."

7. Richard W. Gilsdorf, *The Signs of the Times: Understanding the Church since Vatican II* (Green Bay, Wis.: Star of the Bay, 2008), pp. 88–89, citing *L'Osservatore Romano,* September 29, 1968.

8. See www.stpio.com.

About the Author

BRIAN O'NEEL is a writer and editor in Wisconsin who has spent most of his career in California politics and writing for Catholic magazines. He and his wife are the parents of six children, and Brian's dream is to someday get the whole family to a Green Bay Packers game. His Web site is www.sacredhearttours.com.